Don't Yell challah in a Crowded Matzah Bakery!

The Book of Kosher L'Pesach Humor & Stress Relief

Mordechai Schmutter

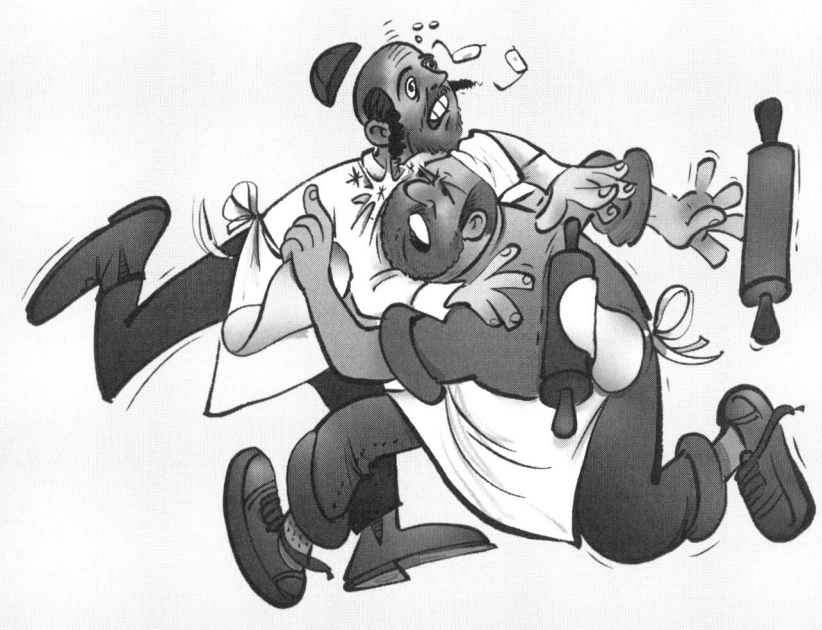

in a Crowded Matzah Bakery!

The Book of Kosher L'Pesach Humor & Stress Relief

Mordechai Schmutter

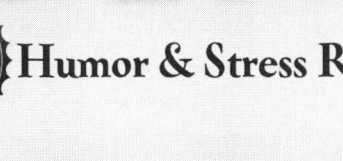

Copyright © 2008 by M. Schmutter

ISBN 978-1-60091-050-0

All rights reserved. No part of this book may be reproduced or transmitted in any form or by any means (electronic, photocopying, recording or otherwise) without prior permission of the copyright holder or distributor.

Book design by:
Sruly Perl
845.371.2222 ext. 106

Questions or comments for the author: imnotreallysure@juno.com

Distributed by:
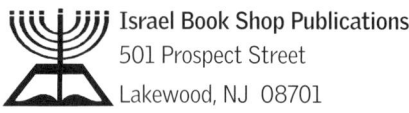 Israel Book Shop Publications
501 Prospect Street
Lakewood, NJ 08701
Tel: (732) 901-3009
Fax: (732) 901-4012
www.israelbookshoppublications.com
info@israelbookshoppublications.com

Printed in Canada

Dedication

To Sara

the only person who can continuously look me in the eye and tell me I'm not funny.

Table of Contents

CHAPTER 1
Chometz and You..15

CHAPTER 2
The Obligatory Products List................................39

CHAPTER 3
Cleaning House..53

CHAPTER 4
The Four Major Food Groups...............................75

CHAPTER 5
The Matzah Factory..91

CHAPTER 6
Recipes for Disaster..103

CHAPTER 7
The Day Before Tomorrow..................................119

CHAPTER 8
Seder Up...139

CHAPTER 9
Funny You Should Ask.......................................155

CHAPTER 10
Talking Up a Storm...171

CHAPTER 11
All That and Food Too..219

CHAPTER 12
The Rest of Pesach...233

CHAPTER 13
It Isn't Over Until About a Week After it's Over...................243

Acknowledgements

There are a lot of people without whom this book would not have been possible, and I plan to reiterate this if there are any lawsuits. Therefore, I would like to thank:

My wife, Sara, who does a lot of work around the house while I sit around and write, and never misses an opportunity to point this out.

My parents, for messing me up just enough that I would write humor, but not enough that I would write nonsense on the walls.

My in-laws, who put up with our strange Passover customs year after year, no matter how often we hint that we would rather just make Pesach at home. And also for allowing a humor writer to marry their daughter in the first place, despite the fact that this painted a huge target on their backs.

Chaim Kaufman, who gave me tons of legal advice before he even passed the bar. And he's not even a book lawyer. I also thank him for happily answering the phone at all hours of the night so that I can make use of his troves of random knowledge, such as the time I called him at eleven-thirty to find out at *exactly* what part of the matzah-baking process one would separate challah.

Josh White, who has tried to jumpstart my writing career on at least four separate occasions.

The people at Hamodia, for continuing to run my humor column week after week, despite the fact that everyone I meet is absolutely shocked that Hamodia even *has* a humor column.

The guys in my shul, for proofreading my writing every week. During davening.

The people at Israel Book Shop, for taking me under their wing, and for not getting annoyed by the fact that I handed in my manuscript an entire year behind schedule.

The Ribbono Shel Olam, for getting me to this point, and for making sure that this year had two Adars, without which I definitely would have missed my deadline again. In fact, I had been pushing for three Adars.

I would also like to thank all of the people who would be offended if I didn't mention them. If not for them, I don't think I would have written this paragraph.

Introduction

Many years ago, our ancestors were enslaved in Egypt, a strange land (the Torah's words, not mine), whose inhabitants wore big snoods and miniskirts (and that was just the *men*). The Egyptians did not believe in G-d; but instead worshipped astrology, cats, firstborns, sheep, the Nile, and a heavily-constipated monarch who insisted that everyone call him "Pharaoh" with an "F."

Our ancestors themselves did not worship any of these things, but instead focused most of their attention on their families, which were huge, because they were having six babies at a time. This made Pharaoh very nervous, and of course he did not remember all of the good things that Yosef had done for Egypt in previous generations. In fact, to conform with the growing anti-Semitism of the time, he ran for king under the platform: "Vote for Pharaoh: He Doesn't Remember Yosef." So he gathered everyone together and forced them to construct government buildings on swampland for two hundred and ten years straight without pay or vacation or any sort of family health plan.

So Hashem brought ten plagues against the Egyptians, smiting them from dawn until dusk until their insides looked like mayonnaise. This all culminated in Pharaoh racing into the Jewish quarter in his royal footsie pajamas in the middle of the night and begging them to leave, while the Jews were holding their very first Seder featuring *matzah* and roasted sheep. (The sheep were glad to die for the cause, because they never really thought of themselves as gods anyway, and it annoyed them that the Egyptians were always coming up to them and asking them for stuff. "No, I can't help you win the lottery. I'm a sheep, for crying out loud!") Their Seder was a lot like the Sedarim we have nowadays, only *Dayenu* was shorter and they had more sons. They also ate *marror* to remind them of the bad days, because that was when they realized that it was all in service of the redemption.

And thus we became a nation.

Of all of the Jewish holidays, one of the most widely celebrated is Passover. Jews whose biggest connection to religion is that their grandparents say "Oy" once in a while nevertheless get together for a Seder every year. Everyone loves Pesach. Yet, at the same time, everyone dreads Pesach. There are very few things in life that you both love and dread at the same time. Your in-laws, for example. Also, Black Friday.

Pesach is very exciting. We have a spiritual, meaningful Seder, as well as a bunch of fun rituals, such as throwing our carbs into a bonfire and holding our *afikoman* for ransom, plus we get to spend time with our relatives. But on the other hand, there are the weeks of cleaning and cooking, and abstaining from foods that we love and know how to make in favor of foods that we have no idea how to prepare properly and don't even taste right if we do. Plus we have to spend time with our relatives. (In the old days, everyone lived with their whole extended family, and the average life expectancy was a lot shorter. This cannot be a coincidence.)

The problem is that the spiritual and exciting aspects of the holiday are often overshadowed by the parts that make us nervous — the parts that, Heaven forbid, lead us to believe that while Pesach is a reminder of our freedom, the weeks before Pesach are a reminder of our slavery.

But do we have to see it that way? Do we have to see it as two different sides of the coin — the good parts of Pesach and the bad parts of Pesach? What if we saw them all as the good parts of Pesach? What if we can find a way to look at the hard work that we have to do in a new light — to see the humor in what we put ourselves through, and to know that we are not alone? And what if we take this bit of humor with us on the job and become a little less stressed?

When something doesn't happen the way we want it to, some part of us knows that some day, after all this is over, we will look back on it and laugh. But you don't need to laugh *after* Pesach. After Pesach is *Sefirah*. You need to laugh right NOW, before you lose it.

And maybe, just maybe, if you turn around after two weeks of cleaning the house and find that the entire time your two year old has been following right behind you and leaving a trail of Cheerios so he can find his way back to civilization, then instead of having a heart attack, your immediate reaction will be to laugh, because it will remind you of a joke.

This book will help.

Or maybe not. Who knows?

Chapter One
Chometz and You

What is *Chometz?*

Simply put, *chometz* is leaven. Leaven is one of those legitimate English words that we only know because we're Jewish, like "tabernacle" and "fortiori." Basically, it involves any of the major grains, i.e. wheat, whole wheat, barley, whole barley, rye, Cheerios, multi-grain Cheerios, and something called spelt. If any of these grains or their derivatives comes into contact with water and is allowed to sit for a good *kabbalistic* length of time such as eighteen minutes, then the mixture will begin rising, and may continue to do so until it has to be subdued with a flamethrower. This is called real *chometz*.

The dough is able to do this because of an ingredient called yeast, which helps it rise. Although most of us are entirely unfamiliar with yeast, except for in those big cubes that look like tofu that the grocer keeps near the milk, it turns out that you don't actually have to buy yeast to make *chometz*. Yeast is a single-celled fungus, like athlete's foot, that is in the air all around us, according to the American Medical Association of Making People Afraid to Breathe. Yeast reproduces by splitting itself in two, until it has millions of children who look exactly like it, which is really good, because the world can be a lonely place for a single-celled fungus. It's nice to at least have some kind of unicellular *nachas*. But it's not easy for a single parent of billions to feed all of those really little mouths, so it feeds them the sugars in your dough, and then nags them about having children of their own once they turn eighteen minutes. The yeasts eat the sugars and produce carbon dioxide, which has nowhere to go because the dough is sticky, and the dough just puffs up like your airbag after you go over a mid-sized pothole.

And you thought your bread machine was so talented.

Chometz on Pesach

The Torah tells us that for the entire week of Pesach we are not allowed to go anywhere near *chometz*. We are not allowed to have it in our possession; we are not allowed to derive any kind of benefit from it; and we are not allowed to poke at it with our ten-foot poles. This is to commemorate the fact that when our forefathers left Egypt they were kicked out so fast that they didn't even have time to pack sandwiches for the trip. (Forty years times three meals a day is a lot of sandwiches.) Not only that, but they did not even have time to make *bread* for the sandwiches. They just threw together some flour and water and tossed it into their carry-on luggage, where it got compressed by all of the other things that they were taking along, and then it baked on their backs in the desert heat, which was hot enough to fry an egg, forming round *matzah*-type crackers that tasted like the inside of a carry-on bag.

Chometz And You

Okay, that last part is not true. In actuality, they found that the *matzos* tasted pretty good, especially with cream cheese, and continued to eat it until Hashem made it start raining takeout, and you don't get food any fresher than that. But the Jews definitely decided that they would not mind eating *matzah* for one week a year, in remembrance.

Way back when, groceries did not sell compressed yeast, and they probably did not sell milk, either. The milkman did. Whereas nowadays many groceries grow large colonies of yeast in their basement storage areas, in those days, people had to actually rely on the natural, free-range yeast floating around. So once they made their dough, it would take forever for enough yeast cells to latch on and raise their kids and grandkids etc. to maturity. It is entirely possible that, if the Jews had made their dough as soon as they got to Egypt, it *still* would not have been ready when it was time to go out. That is the greatness of Pesach.

Therefore, any of the grains that we eat on Pesach must be in the form of *matzah*, or at least machine *matzah*, according to those who feel that the Jews carried around *matzah* machines. This *matzah* must be made from grains that have been *shmura*, or watched, since the time they were cut, but not sooner, since there's nothing more boring or counterproductive than watching wheat grow on a *mashgiach*'s salary. We are also very careful to erect safeguards around anything that may be related to anything that came into contact with anything that can be mistaken for anything within walking distance of *chometz*, because eating *chometz* on Pesach is a crime punishable by death, which will come at the hand of Hashem, because it is very difficult to explain to the non-Jewish media why you're stoning your neighbor for eating a bowl of noodles.

Don't Yell Challah

So we are very careful about keeping anything in our possession that may contain *chometz*, such as the unidentified food items we received in *shalach manos* (more on this later); *matzos* left over from last Pesach (more on this later too, unless I forget); and homemade macaroni necklaces that our children are required by law to make in school when the teacher runs out of craft ideas, and are designed to teach the children important educational lessons such as that school project glue tastes better than uncooked macaroni.

There are a lot of things that may not even be actual food items that are nevertheless questionable or forbidden anyway, because they contain starches, which may or may not include wheat starch. There are countless products that you use every day that you may not even realize would have starch — that have no logical reason to contain starch at all, but the manufacturers throw it in anyway, just to freak us out. Two of the more commonly known products are paper plates, which people do not actually eat, but they do eat *off* of them, and dry-cleaned shirts, which some people also eat off of, but generally not the same people who care about getting their shirts dry-cleaned.

And then there are cigarettes. Many smokers avoid certain brands of cigarettes on Pesach, because of the starches in the paper, which, if they are *chometz*, can incur the death penalty. Although they're totally okay with smoking in the first place. Apparently death is not so bad, so long as you get to choose how you're gonna go.

The Question

The question here is obvious: We eat *matzah* to commemorate the fact that Hashem took us out quickly, and that the Jews back

Chometz And You

then found fresh *matzah* in their luggage. That makes sense. A lot of our holidays are built around which foods best symbolize the story of the holiday. On Rosh Hashana, for instance, Hashem judges whether or not we will have a good year, so we eat honey. On Simchas Torah, we celebrate the annual completion of the reading of the Torah, so we eat stuffed cabbage, which is wrapped like a Torah. On Chanukah, the Jews defeated the Greeks and were able to re-consecrate the Temple and go back to work, so we eat donuts. At least the roots of our eating *matzah* actually have something to do with food.

But why eat it at the exclusion of everything else? Why do we have to throw out all of our bread and our bagels and our kindergarten art projects, and possibly even our shirts? We don't throw out all of our meat before the Nine Days! We don't go around before a fast day throwing out all of our food, even though there is a very real possibility that we could forget at some point during the day and say, "Hey, it's food! Come to think of it, I don't think I've eaten all day!" We don't throw out all of our healthy foods before Chanukah, do we? We don't throw out all of our fresh fruit before Tu Bishvat so that we can eat the dry ones! And why do they have to be dry? What's so bad about eating a little fresh fruit once in a while? And what exactly is a carob?

The Answer

The answer that many commentaries give is that *chometz* represents the *yetzer hara*, or evil inclination. The *yetzer hara* is the little guy who sits on your left shoulder and gives you interesting excuses as to why nothing he's telling you to do is really all that bad, and the people you're doing it to really deserve it, because they did something to you first at the advice of *their yetzer haras*, and so on. There are many ways that *chometz* itself

Don't Yell Challah

is like the evil inclination, one example of which is the sin of falsehood, in the way that a loaf of bread presents itself as being bigger and more substantial than a *matzah*, even though the only difference between the two is hot air. So on Pesach, not only do we have to eat *matzah*, but we also have to stay away from our evil inclinations, which are easy to keep track of because they spend the entire week sitting on our shoulders and complaining about the fact that we can't eat *chometz*.

Yet Another Question

This explanation is all well and good, unless we think about the fact that it's perfectly okay to eat *chometz* the rest of the year! And that's not just the *yetzer hara* talking! There are entire *mitzvos* revolving around *chometz*, such as *challah*, which is also the focal point of the entire Shabbos table. And does this mean that we can never eat donuts?

The Tempting Response

Why do you have to ask so many questions? Never mind why the rules are the way they are! Hashem could have just left us in Egypt, and we would still be working there, although chances are we would not, because at some point Abraham Lincoln would have said something. But that's still a lot of years of slavery and lack of equality, as well as being forever indebted to the leaders of the United States and Egypt for talking it out over a bunch of dead soldiers. Hashem didn't have to take us out of Egypt, but He did anyway, and in the most miraculous ways we could imagine. So is it so much to ask that we just keep quiet and eat our *matzah* without asking so many annoying questions?

Chometz And You

The Actual Answer

Yes. Judaism is all about asking questions. And why not?

Pesach in particular is designed around a Question and Answer model, meaning that we do a lot of strange things on Pesach just so our kids should ask, "Why are we doing this?" Which, if you ask me, is a lot of tuition down the drain. And then we can respond in the way that good Jewish fathers have been answering for thousands of years: "We do this because we want you to ask questions," although studies show that only one in four children is actually satisfied by this answer. But then our children all go on to give the same answers to all of *their* kids, because they never really learn the right ones, and Pesach is all about tradition, anyway.

Yes, we do things so that our children should ask, but we're not actually supposed to tell them that. The kids already know that answer, because it was one of the few things that the teacher actually managed to get through to them before giving them recess so that she could come up with a whole bunch of Passover craft projects that don't involve macaroni. What our children really want to know is, "Why, of all the abnormal things we could possibly do, do we choose these things in particular?" And the correct response is always, "Ask your mother."

Like asking incessant questions, the *yetzer hara* is not necessarily a bad thing. We're supposed to be able to harness its power for good. Falsehood, for example, can sometimes be a good thing, as in the story of Avraham Avinu. When Hashem told Sara that she and Avraham would have a child, Sara laughed and said that her husband was like a hundred years old, which would make him a hundred and forty when it was time to walk their son down the aisle; and then Hashem, when he repeated this to Avraham, said that Sara laughed because she was going to

Don't Yell Challah

give birth at ninety. Although that is really not funny. So Avraham said, "Ninety? How about me? I'm a hundred!" And he did not get angry with Sara. And so we see that Hashem lied to Avraham to preserve peace in the home, and they ended up having a son, instead of getting into a big hairy argument that ended with Avraham having to sleep in the guest tent.

So lying to preserve the peace is a good thing. Therefore, when your boss asks you why you did not come into work yesterday, and you tell him that you were not feeling well when the truth is that you were out skiing, that is okay, because you are really just preserving the peace. So we see that every lie can be excused that way, and it can really get out of hand if not done under the supervision of a highly trained rabbi. In the same way, yeast is a good thing, unless you add too much, in which case your dough will collapse and smell rancid and your husband will ask you about it over the Shabbos table when he notices that he has to cut the *challah* with a jackhammer, and you will have to lie to him if you want to preserve the peace. So we see that once we start lying, it never ends.

Types of *Chometz*

There are many different types of *chometz*, with new ones being invented every day. For instance, when I was a kid I used to think that maybe ink was *chometz*. Ink. Like in a ballpoint pen. I could not imagine what it was made of, and whether or not it involved wheat, or maybe even this "spelt" thing, so I wrote all of my Haggadah notes in pencil. I could actually see the lead in the pencil, and it was solid and definitely did not contain any *chometz*.

Chometz And You

But nowadays, when I look back at my notes and realize that I can't read a word of them because they're all faded, I realize that if ink was *chometz*, what about the ink in all of my *other* notebooks? And my textbooks, with ballpoint beards and moustaches on all of the revolutionaries?

So ink is probably not *chometz*, although we don't know this for sure on any given year until the rabbis look into it. These manufacturers are always trying to sneak *chometz* into everything right under our noses, and it's up to the rabbis to call them up and find out whether this is the year they decided to mess with us on the ink front.

RABBI: "Hello, this is Rabbi Pesach Bookschreiber from New York. I was wondering if your company has changed the ingredients in your ink over the past year."

TOP EXECUTIVE AT INK, INC.: "No, we still just use regular ink. What did you say your name was?"

RABBI: "Rabbi Pesach Bookschreiber. Are you sure you haven't added anything? Something to make your pens stop exploding? Something to make it come out in the laundry?"

TOP EXECUTIVE: "Why do you want to know? Do you work for the competition? You people are asking for another lawsuit!"

RABBI: "I'm just a concerned citizen. What would you say is the likelihood that your ink can be digested by, say, a dog or a small child?"

TOP EXECUTIVE: "What kind of Rabbi did you say you were, again?"

So you can see that this is not an easy job. But it is nevertheless a very important one, because you never know when they're going to stick a lump of dough on the pen one year and call it an eraser. Which begs the question: What exactly are erasers made from? Needless to say, all of the pencil mistakes in my Pesach notebooks are just scribbled over.

Examples Of Items That Are *Chometz*

- Bread crumbs
- Wheaties
- Spelties
- Ravioli
- Fortiori
- Wheat germ
- The sticky stuff at the bottom of your fridge

Examples of items that are not *Chometz* (as of 3:00 this afternoon)

- *Shmura* water
- Ink
- Regular germs
- Your mother

Things People Don't Eat That May or May not be *Chometz*

"It doesn't make sense," a woman is quoted as saying in a Passover issue of the Jerusalem Post. "I'm not a religious woman. Yet on Pesach, all I can eat is *matzah* and jam. While my Iraqi neighbor, a pious rabbi, eats corn, rice and bean salad and finishes it off with a cake made from ground peanuts. Isn't it time that the Jews had one *halacha*, one legal code for everybody?"

Chometz And You

While the question does need to be addressed, we have three responses for this woman:

1. Leave your neighbor alone. He's probably just trying to counter the effects of the *matzah*.
2. Back when there was one legal code for everybody, everybody was religious.
3. Not all of us are allowed to put jam on our *matzah*.

It all boils down to factions. Way back when, all of the Jews lived pretty much in one place, although that place shifted around the desert for forty years. And then they started splitting up. A few people didn't want to enter Israel. A few people didn't like the king, or the prophet, or the relative lack of violent crime, so they moved out. Then the Temple was destroyed, and everyone was chased around for a while. So even though people kept erecting safeguards against violating the prohibition of *chometz*, the chances that everyone would have the same safeguards were pretty slim. Most of the communities were isolated from each other, and there were no phones or Instant Messenger back then:

ONTHERUN613: Is anyone in this chat room?

HIDINGINACAVE248: Hey, ONTHRN! How have you been?

ONTHERUN613: BH, BH. How's Pesach cleaning coming?

HIDINGINACAVE248: Not gr8. There's a lot of dirt down here, and it's dark. U?

ONTHERUN613: I don't have a house at this point. Oh, hey, we just came out with an edict against eating wet *matzah* on Pesach.

HIDINGINACAVE248: LOL. You wanna *daven mincha*?

ONTHERUN613: Not right now. The hordes are coming.

Don't Yell Challah

--- **ONTHERUN613** signed off at 6:32 PM, M.E.S.T. (Middle Eastern Standard Time) ---

So there was very little communication. Even snail mail was unreliable, because everyone's address kept changing. So a lot of Jewish tradition back then was like the childhood Shabbos afternoon game of "Telephone," in which a "leader" whispers a secret code word to the little kid next to him with the cute speech impediment, or, better yet, to the cute children on either side of him, and then those kids whisper it to the kids next to them and so on, until the word goes all the way around both sides of the room, and everyone gets to laugh when the last person on either team repeats aloud the gibberish he or she thinks the leader said. Then they all try to judge which team was more on the money. They can't just ask the leader what word he started with, because he will have long-since gotten bored and wandered off to see if there's any more *chulent*.

Jewish tradition is the same way, but instead of *chulent*, there's persecution, and instead of a secret code word, there are a bunch of complicated laws that are whispered from father to son so that the hordes do not get wind of them. For some of these sons, there was not much they caught besides "...or else we could die." So they all erected whatever safeguards they could think of and hoped it would be enough. So it turns out it's nothing like "Telephone."

A. *KITNIYOS*

One of the most commonly held Passover safeguards is the ban against *kitniyos*, or anything that can be confused with, or has derivatives that can be confused with, any of the major grains. Rice, for example, looks a lot like grain to most of us, who have

Chometz And You

never seen an actual stalk of wheat in real life. It can be made into rice flour, which could be mistaken for real flour; and it can be made into rice milk, once you figure out how to milk a rice kernel, and can then be confused with cow's milk, although that doesn't really matter as far as Pesach is concerned. Also, nowadays everything is clearly labeled. But the point is that rice is very versatile. And almost everything that's versatile and not already *chometz* falls into the category of *kitniyos*. That is why tofu is *kitniyos*, thank G-d.

Other examples of *kitniyos* include: groats, millet, *kimmel*, fennel, funnel, the Chunnel, corn, peas, peas and corn, baby corn, corn on the cob, peanuts, beans, green beans, string beans, jelly beans, caraway, poppy, sesame, Everything, linseed, cotton, and buckwheat, which is apparently not a wheat.

Also, based on our current definition of *kitniyos* as anything that could be confused with *chometz*, it turns out that potatoes are *kitniyos* too, for the very reason that we put it into almost everything on Pesach by means of potato starch. Potato starch looks a lot like wheat flour, until you actually try to bake it into a pastry and find that it doesn't rise and it sticks to the roof of your mouth, and that it's not really that much better than just baking the eggs and the sugar. (Although it *is* better than putting whole potatoes into your sponge cake.) This may come as a shock to you if you've spent every Pesach since you were born peeling potatoes and trying to think of new things to do with them for the twenty-four meals of Pesach and having dreams midway though Pesach wherein you are attacked by a giant potato holding a ten-foot peeler, but before you run into the garage and blowtorch your head you should know that potatoes are still okay.

Back when our rabbinical leaders were deliberating the fate of rice flour and buckwheat flour and baby powder, there was

Don't Yell Challah

no such thing as potatoes. Sure, potatoes existed over in South America, but we didn't know about them, so they didn't exist. Kind of like the Americas themselves. So the rabbinical ban never included them. Of course, it never included corn, which also grew in the Americas, but the rabbis decided that any new foods they would find could be added to the ban as necessary. And then potatoes were introduced into Europe. That was a great day for the Jews. They danced far into the night.

Potatoes, as it turns out, were very easy to grow, as many of us have proven in grade school by jabbing toothpicks into them and hanging them over a jar of water on our windowsills and watching as they sprouted enormous potato vines and fell into the sink. So even though the Jews had nothing to eat back then and were always getting chased out of villages, they found they were always able to run around with their little jars of water. But then Pesach came along, and they realized that if they declared potatoes *kitniyos*, they'd have nothing to eat, and they decided it was far better to have nothing to eat besides potatoes. And poor man's bread was expensive. So the rabbis just never added potatoes to the ban.

So in the end, anyone whose ancestors came from the potato-infested regions of Europe are allowed to eat potatoes on Pesach, and anyone whose ancestors came from regions infested with other products such as oil did not have to worry about it either, because they never came up with the laws of *kitniyos* in the first place. Probably they had better product labeling. These people, or "Sefardim" as they are called, had very little communication with the potato people, or "Ashkenazim," so they came up with their own set of Passover safeguards, which involved checking their rice kernels individually upwards of twenty times each, so that over the

Chometz And You

course of the holiday, the average Sefardi family was able to eat almost an entire handful of rice.

As for the history of the Ashkenazi-Sefardi split, I would like to say that, thanks to years of extensive education at some of the finest *yeshivas* around, I have no idea how that came about. *Yeshivas* don't really teach Jewish history. Once Moshe dies, it's all pretty much guesswork. But from the bits and pieces that I *do* know, thanks to the time the assistant principal substituted my math class and drew pictures of Eurasia on the board while we all made faces at his back, I was able to glean the following questionable information:

"*Ashkenaz*" means Germany, and "*Sefard*" means Spain. Obviously, this has very little to do with where we actually come from.

Ashkenazim these days come from all over Eastern Europe, Russia, and strangely, Great Britain. So apparently the Ashkenazi-Sefardi split was not the last split we've had thus far.

Ashkenazim invented a language called Yiddish, which encompasses Hebrew, German, and the word "Oy." Sefardim invented a language called Ladina, which may or may not be Latino.

During the Inquisition of 1492, the Spanish Jews were scattered, and a lot of them settled into the Arab countries, which was widely regarded as a bad move.

Columbus was Jewish, and figured out how to use the fact that the King of Spain wanted to get him out of the country to get an all-expenses paid Pesach vacation to the Bahamas.

He was the only Jew in history named Christopher.

Don't Yell Challah

B. *GEBRUKTZ*

Another popular safeguard among many Chassidic communities, as well as people who have Chassidic blood in them and who know this primarily because they don't eat *gebruktz*, is *gebruktz*. *Gebruktz*, which literally means broken pieces of *matzah*, actually refers to *matzah* that has become wet in some way. An extreme example of this is *matzah* balls, which are made from broken pieces of *matzah*, which are made wet by the *matzah* ball ingredients, and again by the big pot of water you cook them in, and then again when you put them into your soup. So for anyone who does not eat *gebruktz*, that's a quadruple heart attack right there.

Gebruktz originated back when everyone made his own *matzah*, and every single person had this little fear in the back of his mind that, if he made it himself, then it was probably *chometz*. What if he did something wrong? What if he forgot one of the five hundred laws of *matzah* baking? What if some of the flour in the *matzah* did not get baked properly? It did not help that this was the only time of the year that men tried their hands at baking. So the Rabbis decreed that everyone should be careful around the *matzos*, just in case.

This is very ironic, as most of the Jewish world looks forward to Passover mainly for the *matzah* balls, while, for many Orthodox Jews, this is the one week a year that we *don't* eat them. Try explaining that to your irreligious coworkers. "No, we don't eat *matzah* balls on Pesach." "Then what's the point?" they ask.

I myself hold of the ban against *gebruktz*, and do not even put jam on my *matzah*. If I want a sandwich, I take a bite of *matzah*, and then wash it down with a spoonful of jam, which is actually not that bad. But next year, everyone in the house is going to get his own jar. But people who do eat *gebruktz* cannot believe that I can survive for an entire week without *matzah* meal. "What about *matzah brei*?" they ask. "You don't know what you're missing!" To be honest, I have never personally tasted *matzah brei*, so I actually *don't* know what I'm missing. But I have to wonder why, if it's so good, how come no one tries to get me to eat it the rest of the year? I have a similar philosophy with potato starch. You don't see anyone eating potato starch pancakes on Chanukah.

Other, lesser known Pesach safeguards include:

C. FISH

This is another Chassidic custom. Many people do not eat fish on Passover, because there was a time that fishermen used to pack their fish in *chometz* alcohol, probably so that their wives would stop asking them how come they came home from *every* fishing trip smelling like a winery. Instead, a lot of them make a "false" fish out of chicken. So when you find a piece of what looks like fried fillet in their homes, you should really check, especially if you are a Yekke of Germanic descent (as opposed to an Ashkenazy, apparently). This is because some Yekkes don't eat:

D. CHICKEN

Chickens eat corn, which is *kitniyos*, and they don't even bother to check them twenty times for wheat kernels. Apparently the Yekkes were cutting open chickens and finding semi-digested wheat, which totally irked them, being Yekkish and all, and so they decided to put a stop to it altogether. One has to wonder what one would eat if his father was Chassidic and his mother was a Yekke, although chances are that this would never happen, as his grandparents would never have come to a conclusion over the issue of whether to have the wedding two hours late or strictly on time. (That joke is older than both Chassidim *and* Yekkes.) We're guessing these Yekkes make a "false" chicken out of fish, which, oddly enough, is the one thing you can't get to taste like chicken.

Also, some people don't eat:

E. SMOKED MEAT OR LOX

And we don't know why. It probably has something to do with alcohol.

F. GARLIC

Some people don't eat garlic on Pesach, because once upon a time they used to store it with wheat. Another reason for the garlic prohibition is that many of the Passover traditions revolve around talking to your children, and they are far less likely to listen if you have garlic breath. **(THIS IS NOT A JOKE. I saw this in a reliable publication. Really.)**

G. TOOTHPASTE

Just kidding, I hope.

H. CARROTS

Many communities stay away from carrots, because the Yiddish word for carrot, as we know from the Rosh Hashanah honey-dipping fest, is *merin*, which is similar to the Hebrew word *me'arah*, which means dough (as in *Me'aras Hamachpeilah*). Needless to say, Sefardim who have never accepted Yiddish don't hold of this tradition either, and that is a good thing, because they need to keep up their vision for checking rice.

Chometz And You

I. BAGGIES

Don't be silly. *Nobody* eats baggies. But there are some people who hold of *gebruktz* to the extent that they actually eat their *matzah* over little plastic baggies, which they discard, and only then do they bring out the rest of the meal. There are probably also people who spend the entire Pesach in little plastic bubbles, breathing *shmura* air and eating nothing but *matzah*. They do have fun on their Chol Hamoed trips, though, bouncing around the zoo in those bubbles.

The Situation Nowadays

Once we hit the modern era and everyone was able to communicate again, the Jewish people wasted no time intermarrying between the different sects, to the point where we have reached a stalemate wherein no two people actually have the same Passover customs. This can cause problems, especially for Siamese twins, so to make things less complicated, many of us have adopted a custom against "*mishing*," or eating in other people's homes for the whole of Pesach. This custom has worked out very well for generations of Jewish men, who are looking for any excuse not to spend Pesach with the in-laws. "We don't *mish*," they proudly announce. They then proceed to get into a heated argument with their wives over whether they will therefore be spending Pesach over at *his* parents' house or just staying home and feeling guilty.

And then there are people like me. I don't eat *gebruktz*; I don't eat smoked meat or lox or garlic or plastic bags; and I definitely don't *mish*, even in the sense of eating foods prepared by actual food companies. Yet I still find myself over at my in-laws' house every other year. We sit at the far end of the table and eat the

Don't Yell Challah

"special" (as in "My Mommy says I'm special") foods that my mother-in-law prepares for us wrapped in eighty-five layers of silver foil, so that you think you're about to eat a baked potato, but by the time you finish unwrapping it you discover that it's a grape. And then all of the other years we go over to *my* parents' house, and find out about yet another food that we have to tell my mother-in-law that we don't eat, because when you're a kid growing up in your parents' house and your mother doesn't serve something like quinoa for the whole week of Pesach, you don't think, "maybe we don't eat this on Pesach," you just count your blessings.

For instance, last year I found out that we don't eat lox. I had never noticed this before. I thought that the main reason my parents never served lox on Pesach is because we never had bagels on Pesach. There were plenty of other weeks throughout the year that we did not have lox, and I didn't give those any thought either. Maybe I should have. But my mother-in-law, who does not like the idea of us coming over to her house and starving for eight days because she thinks it decreases the likelihood that we're going to come back the next time, went ballistic.

"It's just fish!" she said. "You eat fish!"

"As far as I know," I said. "So far. But don't worry about it. We don't come here for the food. We come here for the scintillating conversation. Like this one right now."

"But why don't you eat lox?"

"I don't know," I said. "We just don't."

This really got to her. My mother-in-law comes from a family whose tradition it is to eat almost anything on Pesach that is not actually bread, and when she got married, my father-in-law decided to abide by her customs, which made life easier for them,

Chometz And You

because they live out in the sticks. There are actual sticks in their backyard. There's that, coupled with the fact that her chosen profession is "food scientist," coupled still with the fact that she runs a kosher food information website that I would not blatantly advertise for except for the fact that she is reading this book and I've been making fun of her for at least a page now. (WWW.KASHRUT.COM. She specializes in Passover food labeling alerts.) So she cannot fathom why I would blindly accept a tradition for which: A. I do not know the reason. B. Chances are that any possible reason no longer applies nowadays, and C. Is scientifically the same as another food that I *do* eat on Pesach. And it is very hard to argue with her, because she is a food scientist.

For instance, every year she tries to get me to eat Hershey's baking chocolate. Needless to say, I don't eat Hershey's baking chocolate on Passover. Even during the year, I can go for weeks without thinking about it. And for the week of Pesach, I don't even eat baking chocolate made by *Jewish* brands. What I do eat is Jewish brands of cocoa powder; the kind with no nutritional value that is produced by companies known more for their lines of candy. This is because another tradition we have is one against eating foods produced by non-Jewish brands, I guess on the theory that these people cannot possibly understand the seriousness of Pesach, and might decide to make it festive by adding *matzah* balls. To their baking chocolate.

"All the brands are made in the same plant," she reminds me, year after year. "I know the *mashgiach*."

"There has to be some difference," I say, trying to hide the fact that I have absolutely no idea what I'm talking about. "They certainly *taste* different from each other," I add, because that is the extent of my knowledge of food.

Don't Yell Challah

"But then how about *Jewish* baking chocolate?" my mother-in-law argues, pulling out her books. "Baking chocolate is made out of cocoa, which you eat, and margarine, which you eat, and sugar, which you also eat!"

"I think it's because of *mishing*," I usually say. Then I say something along the lines of her being able to put those same three ingredients together herself, seeing as she's a food scientist and all. And then she pulls out her trump card.

"Eating cocoa powder is *mishing* too, you know."

So I usually lose the argument. But that doesn't mean I eat the chocolate. Because it's not about me, it's about tradition.

I realize that my traditions may seem crazy to you, the reader, but then you probably have traditions that seem crazy to other people. For instance, outside of Israel, there is no such thing as a one-day *yom tov*. Everything has at least two days. This dates back to the times when the beginning of the month was judged by when the moon was first seen, and sometimes it took upwards of three months to let everyone know that it was *Rosh Chodesh*, especially those who lived outside of Israel. So the Rabbis decided to institute two-day holidays, so that at least one of them would be the correct date. But nowadays, what with cars and helicopters and all-terrain vehicles, it should not take *nearly* as long to announce a new month. Also, we have phones. And *Rosh Chodesh* is decided by the guy who prints the calendars. So we really have no need for the second day, except to rest up from cooking for a two-day *yom tov*. So, as we understand it, there should no longer be a need for two-day holidays. Nevertheless we're not about to say anything.

But whatever you do, never come right out and tell your mother-in-law to put a food together herself.

What Sect Are You? A Scientific Quiz.

Chometz And You

Take this test to determine which sect you most likely belong to. If you already know your sect, then you should probably skip this quiz, because chances are you're going to be offended.

1. What do you wear to *shul* on Shabbos?

  a. A long coat, an even longer belt, and a dead animal shaped like a donut.

  b. My Shabbos t-shirt, of course. And my white on white on white *tallis*.

  c. Hat, jacket, and tie. My husband wears the same.

2. On the *bentschers* you gave out at your wedding, which name comes first?

  a. The bride

  b. The groom

  c. The caterer

3. Grammatically speaking, what is your biggest pet peeve?

  a. The fact that the word "*hee*" is both male and female possessive.

  b. The fact that nobody knows what a *Jhimmel* is.

  c. The fact that the last letter of the *aleph bet* is the same whether or not it has a dot. What's the point?

4. What is your favorite song of all time?

  a. Yoy doy doy, Yoy doy dum, by Rebbe and the Table Thumpers

  b. Yo Ya, by Why Does Everyone Assume I Like *Yo Ya* Just Because I'm Sefardi?

  c. Yo Yo Yo, by Various Artists

How To Score:

Don't Yell Challah

Tally up all of your answers, giving yourself one point for every time you answered A, two points for B, and three points for C. Depending on how many points you have, you are either some kind of Chassid, some kind of Sefardi, or something else entirely. If your big question is how come I only incorporated these three sects out of the hundreds out there, than you may be Yeshivish. And if you actually took the time to tally up your score, then you're definitely a Yekke.

Is Dirt Chometz?

This question has been raging for centuries, mainly between the sects called "men" and "women," and with good reason. Dirt can be *kitniyos*, because you can confuse it with flour, or at least whole-wheat flour. And it was definitely around back when they established the ban on *kitniyos*. Dirt can get into any place that *chometz* can, and seems to gather primarily on the floors of high food areas, like the kitchen, as well as food storage areas, like the garage or the basement.

But the truth is that dirt is not *chometz*. If it were, why do you suppose that, on the very first Passover, the Jews headed straight for the desert?

Chapter Two
The Obligatory Products List

Aside from the aforementioned categories of: A. Items That Are *Chometz*, and B. Items That Were Not *Chometz* As Of 3:00 The Day I Wrote This, there is a third category of: Items That Are A Little Bit Of Both, But Not Enough Of Either. These items are Hashem's way of keeping people in touch with their rabbis. Sure, the rabbi gives a speech every week, and he periodically reminds you not to talk during *davening*, but it's important to have enough of a relationship with your rabbi so that you feel comfortable asking him embarrassing personal questions, such as what to do if you've just dropped your very last dairy spoon into the chicken soup again, or whether or not you can go to the *mikvah* in your toupee, and the ramifications of it coming off and scaring the first-timers. As such, Hashem has created numerous situations in which you really have no choice but to approach your rabbi, thereby building a give-and-take relationship, in which he gives you guidance at all hours of the day and night, and you give him *shalach manos* come Purim time.

The third category is, in some ways, the most complex of the lot. Some items are only *chometz* if made by certain companies, who do things like put oatmeal in baby wipes for reasons known only to baby wipe scientists, who probably just really like oatmeal. Other items contain *chometz* for more sane reasons, but have special circumstances that allow us to keep them in our possession anyway, such as that our doctors say that we have to keep them around, or our dogs flat out refuse to eat them.

I am referring here to a rabbinic standard when it comes to certain types of *chometz*, which is called "*raui l'achilas kelev*," meaning that a dog to be named later has to be willing to eat it. The rabbis have long since determined that any *chometz* that meets the *kashrus* standards that dogs use, can, under the right circumstances, be used to make regular human dough rise, while anything they refuse to touch would probably just get up and walk away from the dough on its own, or else just eat the dough.

Some people adopt very liberal standards as to what a dog will not eat, despite the fact that their only real experience with dogs is with the one that barks at them from behind a fence on the way to *shul* that causes them to jump so high that they suddenly find themselves on the other side of the street. Nevertheless, they declare: "a dog wouldn't eat this" about almost everything: leftovers, tuna sandwiches, and any food that's room temperature. But in fact most dogs will eat just about anything, including craft projects, on the theory that if it turns out not to be food, they can always throw it up later. And I have a brother who once ate stick deodorant. He was two at the time, and we assume he thought it was white chocolate or something, but when he got up from his

The Obligatory Products List

nap the stick was lying on the bed, almost finished, and there were little teeth marks in it. His breath smelled amazing.

And this is aside from the fact that standards have changed over the years. For instance, back when they decided that dogs were a good measuring stick, *all* foods were room temperature. There was no ice cream in those days, just cream. And three hours later, it was sour cream. It only went downhill from there. It is just like how the standards are different in other parts of the world. Take sushi, for example. Up until Jewish caterers got the idea to serve it at *bar mitzvahs*, sushi was strictly a Japanese food. The Japanese eat a lot of fish, and sometimes when they wake up in the middle of the night looking for something to snack on, they don't want to have to start thawing and baking and so on, so they just eat it raw, straight out of the container, covered in the eight pieces of rice left over from the time they had Chinese. But to everyone else, it was raw fish. And we were raised to believe that raw fish had bacteria (like little yeasts) that could only really be destroyed through exposure to intense heat, followed by horseradish. But the Japanese don't understand how come we're so worried about bacteria, but will nevertheless shake hands with people we've never met. So they bow to each other instead. We bow only to Hashem, while everyone else gets to enjoy our hand bacteria.

The point is that years ago, there was no such thing as bacteria, or at least no one knew about it, besides for the dogs, who stayed up late every night barking at what everyone thought was nothing. So people's standards were more relaxed in those days, and although they didn't live as long, they made decisions based on the standards at the time. And at the time, people ate a cow until there was none left. Red meat wasn't a problem back then; green meat was more of an issue. At that point it was time for the dogs to take over, until the meat developed a lifestyle of its own and started actually attacking the dogs, at which point the rabbis declared that it was no longer *raui l'achilas kelev*.

It is because of these complicated and ever-changing issues that the Jewish Publishing Industry of People Who Actually Know What They're Talking About has to put out updated books *every* year containing detailed information on *every* questionable item with typos. The more up-to-date the book is, the more typos there will be. That's how we know it's up-to-date. These books are put out by rabbis who obsess over Passover all year long and hound product developers over the phone while you're trying to figure out how to get honey out of the *shofar*. These Rabbis are very knowledgeable, as they always paid attention in science class even though they knew they were going to become rabbis, and so they know how to pronounce the names of thousands of chemical compounds, and which ones mean wheat.

As opposed to us. But that's why our list is shorter.

A

Alphabet Soup: This is *chometz*. I don't even know why it's on the list. Probably because I needed something that started with A. (Although don't expect me to hit *every* letter, because there is no way I can find a questionable product that starts with "X." I did find something for "Q" though. But *every* time I think about "X" my mind goes to "xylophone." Thanks a *lot*, Doctor Seuss.)

B

Baby Food: Thanks to the wonderful kindness Hashem bestows upon new mothers, possibly to make up for waking them up in the middle of the night, most babies are born without teeth. As

The Obligatory Products List

such, many of them find it difficult to eat most of the foods eaten by people *with* teeth, such as *matzah*, and gummy worms. So they eat pretty much the same foods as the old people who keep separate meat and dairy teeth, such as yogurt and bananas and seltzer. (Here's a fun experiment: Try feeding your baby seltzer.) But there are only so many bananas a baby can eat before it totally stops needing to be changed, ever. So many companies sell jars of baby food, into which they strain vegetables that no one would ever eat voluntarily, except maybe on Pesach when there's really nothing else, such as zucchini. If no one ate zucchini, farmers would stop growing it, and then where would that portion of our taxes go, huh? So the companies put together little jars with labels that say things like, "Zucchini Beet Prune Bukser Medley," which you have to feed to your baby with a tiny, padded, mental asylum spoon, again because they have no teeth, and because if you use a regular spoon, you might come to notice that you just paid a dollar fifty for what is essentially only about two bites.

The problem is that there are many such companies, and not all of them are Passover friendly. Some of them outright put *chometz* ingredients into their baby food, apparently because someone goofed on an order and they have eight thousand tons of oat stubble lying around, so why not? And some of these companies just make their foods on *chometz* equipment that one week a month they reconfigure the cookie machine to strain asparagus or something. So we have to be really careful about what we buy, unless we want to sell our children to our non-Jewish neighbors along with our pets. (See the section on pet food below, where we discuss how some pet foods are made on *chometz* equipment, probably on the weeks they're not doing baby food.)

If buying Pesach baby food becomes difficult, or we are entirely too freaked out now to even trust labels anymore, one viable option is to actually make our own baby food. Just find any fruit or vegetable that you have lying around the house that you bought when it was on sale, but that no one really wants to eat, ("Wow, eight rutabagas for a dollar! Let's stock up!") and boil the tar out of it until it achieves roughly the same consistency as mayonnaise. Drain out the water, and then squash it with a potato masher, or, if for some reason you don't have a Pesach'*dik* potato masher, you can use the old-time wine straining method, taking care to remove all unwanted toenails and sock lint afterward. Then simply spoon it into baby-food sized jars. The average banana should fill about eleven of these jars. And if you do this all year, you can save a lot of money in the long run, unless you count the medical bills and the therapy. Another option is to feed your baby some more grown-up foods of which it is easier to keep track of their Passover status, such as olive spread or babaganush. Or straight mayonnaise, for that matter.

Another Passover issue when it comes to babies, besides for the oatmeal in the baby wipes (which I was not kidding about, by the way; some companies do put it in, the same way health spas stick it into that spread they serve with the cucumbers) is formula. Because babies are mainly stuck eating things like yams and barley cereal, they don't get many of the nutrients that are essential for the growth of a healthy child, such as orange soda. So companies such as Enfamil, Similac, Isomil, Soyolac, Soyomil, Isolac, and that Israeli one — Petel for Babies, or something — make a "formula" that contains everything that is really essential for the growth of a baby, plus one ingredient that smells weird and makes the babies throw up, all ground up into powder. And apparently one of these ingredients, probably the regurgitant, is *kitniyos*. So the general practice is to give our children the formula anyway, but to serve it out of the bathroom sink, or, if we have major first-time-parent issues with this, to use the garden hose out back.

The Obligatory Products List

C

Candles: In general, most candles are okay. It's not like you're going to eat them anyway. But this ruling holds no bearing on the wax gum they used to make that was shaped like vampire teeth, which turned into tiny pieces of wax when we first bit into it, and then eventually turned into something resembling chewing gum after about fifteen minutes of chewing. I was really into that gum as a kid, and spent many happy hours choking on it. I think it might be illegal now. The companies tried to make us think it was gum, but really it was just wax. It's like the rubber band companies going, "Here, chew on this for a while. It's gum!" That would be the next logical step, now that they've pretty much monopolized the dental industry.

There were also these long wax tubes filled with a bright neon liquid — maybe a half-ounce total — that you never felt had enough liquid, so you chewed on the wax like a cupcake tin when you were done. Those have disappeared too, strangely enough. But for some reason we still have the candy buttons that come on those long strips of toilet paper, where you have to swallow most of the paper along with the candy. But, in general, nowadays we have candies that are legally much safer, and just as much fun, such as "crazy hair" which is basically sweet play dough that comes out the top of a little plastic head, which you then lick off. This goes a long way toward helping you get your kid to sit still in the barber's chair. Other fun things we have are Lego bricks that you're actually *supposed* to eat, lollypops with wads of used gum inside, and gumballs containing a half an ounce of neon liquid in the middle.

There may, however, be some issues with colored candles, which use some of the same food colorings as all of these candies,

Don't Yell Challah

such as Red #35, which has almost as much *kitniyos* as Red #36. So one should try to avoid using Chanukah candles on Pesach. Also, if you are making a birthday party on Pesach, you should try to avoid putting candles in the cake altogether, although that would not be a good idea in the first place because potato starch sponge cake isn't as solid as one would hope, and the candles would just sink right in.

D

Dog Food: May not be *"raui l'achilas kelev."* See *Pet Foods*.

F

Fruit: Not that there's anything wrong with fruit, but some people are careful not to eat fruit peels on Pesach, because you never know who touched them, and whether or not they washed their hands way out in the orchards since the last time they ate *chometz*. I don't know about you, but this logic makes me hesitant to eat fruit peels *ever*. The biggest issue of all is with oranges, which are basically just covered in spray paint. As it turns out, most oranges do not naturally attain that perfect orange color, which does serve to explain why orange juice is actually yellow. The orange coloring is sprayed on by food scientists (not my mother-in-law) using chemicals that may or may not be *chometz*, and actually may be toxic in large doses. So people who refrain from eating peels on Pesach should probably stay away from candied orange peels also, which is just as well, because candied orange peels are an acquired taste, and everyone knows that candy should not have to be an acquired taste. (But if you really crave orange peels, you can probably buy juice oranges, some of which do not have the coloring, and are readily identifiable by

The Obligatory Products List

their cheap price and their yellowish color and brownish specks. You can eat those peels if you'd like.) On Pesach, however, many people refrain from eating any peels at all, and look very funny munching away at whole naked apples on their Chol Hamoed trips. Also, it takes them twenty minutes to eat a grape.

I

Insecticides: You probably shouldn't have any bugs in your house at all over Pesach, what with all that cleaning you just did, not to mention all of the toxic cleansers that were wafting around the house all month that almost put your gerbil into a coma. But let's say that for some reason you *do* have pests, such as that you live in a swamp, or the subway, or you have a small boy living at home whose pockets you forgot to empty once or twice. Your first instinct would be to use bug spray, using the "Empty Half A Can On The Few Bugs That You See Until They Stop Moving" method, which has proven to be at least the most physically satisfying tactic in the past, on the theory that, even if there were somehow *chometz* in the insecticide, it is probably not *chometz* that a dog would eat. But that is only because the dog would not have built up a tolerance to it, unlike the bugs, which seem to be running around under the constant stream of spray even while you're starting to feel woozy. The bugs eat these sprays for breakfast, although first making sure to filter out the mites.

The other option is to use baited traps, but you have to be careful about those, because some of the bait is *chometz*. It's not like the traps are using *matzah* or baked potatoes. Combat Roach Killer, for example, uses oatmeal. Just like baby wipes! You have to wonder what it does for the roaches' complexions. Raid Ant and Roach Killer, meanwhile, uses peanut butter, perhaps on the theory that bugs are allergic. Peanut butter is, of course, *kitniyos*, so you may want to set those traps up in the bathroom, although the truth is there is no such thing as *kitniyos* for bugs anyway, because they're too small to confuse the different types of grains. That's like you confusing two different types of buildings.

M

Medicine: Nobody takes medicine because they like the way it tastes, with the possible exception of Advil. Also bubble gum medicine, which is great with sponge cake. If we did like the taste of acetaminophen, for example, we wouldn't bother eating a whole bowl of them, as we could just as easily substitute something that tastes basically the same, such as soap, or possibly stick deodorant (I'd have to ask my brother). But then none of this matters in terms of Passover, so long as you're putting the medicine in your mouth. You could also claim that medication is the one thing that dogs will not indiscriminately wolf down, but you don't really know that, do you? People don't eat them either, unless they need to. It is possible that if a dog had any notion of cause and effect, it, too, would take A.D.D. medications, or Prozac, or even antacids to help with some of the crazy stuff it eats. So it's a shame that the people in charge of understanding and adding various starches to medications as adhesives or fillers or whatever are not the same people who are concerned about starch in their pills for one week per year.

It is for this reason that Pesach books and magazines come out with long medicine lists every year, along with a disclaimer that you are not to go solely by the list, but are to ask a competent rabbi, who will begin judging your case by consulting the list. I was planning on reading through the list and taking note of any funny or amusing medicine names that I could find, and print them here for your viewing pleasure, but I did not do so for two reasons:

The Obligatory Products List

It is a very long list with a lot of big words, and I suspect that nobody, not even the editor, made it all the way through the list. Maybe if they'd added some jokes or something.

They say that if you make fun of medications you may eventually need to take them yourself, and it would not suit me in the least if everyone who read this book suddenly developed, say, fin rot.

P

Pet Food: We have thus far covered rodents that crawl out of holes in your walls and have babies in your pajama drawer, but we have not spoken about the rodents that look exactly the same that you paid good money for and keep in a cage lined with yesterday's Hamodia. Basically you can feed them vegetables, without the peels of course, or else you can just throw a peanut butter trap into their cage.

As for other kinds of pets, there are only a couple of companies that make kosher for Passover pet foods, which many rabbis are hesitant to put their certification on, because even without the grain additives, it is still basically horsemeat. But they're okay for animals, though. One of these brands actually advertises that they also don't put dairy products into their meat foods, and hosts a whole website that includes kosher pet accessories, such as the *Matzah* Ball Doggie Chew Toy, although you'd think chewing *matzah* itself would be enough. If you can't get your hands on one of these brands, (who so far did not pay me to mention their names), then you really have to come up with *something*, because you don't want to know what eight days of straight *matzah* will do to your dog. There's always table scraps, though. Let's hope your dog likes quinoa.

Don't Yell Challah

Some people, however, choose to avoid the entire headache in the first place by giving their animals to a non-Jewish neighbor, although all that barking at being in a strange house does go a long way toward contributing to anti-Semitism.

As far as tropical fish go, fish flakes are out of the question, because anything that can be made into flakes just *has* to be *chometz*, so a lot of people give them tiny freeze-dried worms that turn into regular worms in water, just like the three pieces of freeze-dried corn that come in instant soup, which, when you pour water on them, also taste like regular worms. But do not be surprised if your fish don't go for the worms, because that may be how some of them came to be in a fish tank in the first place.

Q

Quinoa: When I mentioned quinoa in the previous section about half of you went, "Huh?" As well you should. Quinoa is a vegetable-slash-protein-slash-small grainy thing that my mother-in-law tries to foist on me every Pesach, despite the fact that it very clearly falls into the category of, "If It's So Good, Where Is It The Rest Of The Year?" Quinoa grows naturally in South America, and was only introduced into North America in the 1980s. Airport security was more lax back then. Nowadays they'd never let it pass.

"What did you say this was?" they'd ask, at gunpoint.

"It's quinoa," you'd say.

"Is that an Arab name?" they'd ask suspiciously.

"No," you'd say reassuringly. "It's a vegetable-slash-protein-slash-small grainy thing. It's really good."

"Well, if it's so good," they'd say, "where was it until now?"

The Obligatory Products List

Although it seems similar to rice, quinoa is actually a member of the Goosefoot family, which includes spinach and beets. (I love it when food is related. I picture the other vegetables coming over to it at parties — health food parties, no doubt — and going, "Oh, you're a Goosefoot! Are you related to spinach and beets?") So because quinoa has all these connections, many people are okay with serving it on Pesach.

But as with almost everything regarding the holiday, quinoa is actually the subject of dispute as of 3:00 the day I wrote Chapter One. There are those who say that it is actually *kitniyos*, for the same reason that potatoes should be and corn actually is: because it looks like grain, and it's not nearly as vital as potatoes were in Europe. They want to know what it is with us that we have to find something small and grainy to eat no matter what. Do we miss living in the desert that much?

So I probably don't eat quinoa. Whatever.

R

Redundancies: See *Redundancies*.

T

Toothpaste: Toothpaste is yet another product that heavily depends on which company makes it, so you have to be very careful to check. Or you can just face up to the fact that you only really brush once or twice a month anyway, and avoid the question altogether. But chances are that if you look through your Pesach boxes, you'll find the full tube from last year. And even though dogs don't let toothpaste into their mouths unless you force them to, the truth is that a lot of children do swallow toothpaste.

My two-year-old son, for example, makes me stop brushing his teeth after I finish only the bottom ones (I start with the bottom ones because they are easier to get to, seeing as how I am taller than him), so that he can swallow it all. Then he says "more," and I have to load up the brush again for the top teeth. Maybe I should stop buying toothpaste that tastes like Red Hots. But many small children do the same thing anyway, even with toothpaste that tastes like toothpaste. But it's kind of depressing to know that your kid eats something that a dog would not.

Z

Zebra: Zebras are not kosher, but they are definitely not *chometz*. So if it comes down to it, you can have a zebra carcass in your house over Pesach. It's nice that some things are black and white like that.

Chapter Three
Cleaning House

The Dread

Holidays are funny. They're created to celebrate happy events, i.e. Pesach commemorates the birth of our nation; Purim celebrates the fact that our nation was not all killed out; the day after Thanksgiving celebrates the fact that electronics and office supplies are on sale at five in the morning; and some random day in February commemorates the birthday of a president who died a long time ago. (Call me crazy, but I think that once you die, you should forfeit the right to have people make a big deal about your birthday.) Yet as joyous as these holidays are *supposed* to be, there's always something people dread about them, be it having to put up with relatives who live far away for a reason; or the fact that you will be stuck behind a long line of bargain hunters falling asleep standing up so that you're left standing there with your free-after-rebates laminator under your arm until way after Chanukah;

Don't Yell Challah

or the fear that someone you met once and didn't really like will give you *mishloach manos* and you won't be able to retaliate with one of your three hundred ready-made baskets because all of the names are already laminated on. And instead of focusing on the happiness of the holiday, we always focus on the stress that comes with it.

One of the most stressful points of all of the holidays, the point to which all of the other holidays can only aspire, is cleaning for Pesach. Sure, we all realize the importance of the *mitzvah*, as well as the fact that cleaning the house for Pesach symbolizes rebirth in the same way that our nation was "born" when we left Egypt, but mention Pesach to the average housewife and she will break into a cold sweat and start unconsciously scrubbing something. Many housewives have had that dream wherein they're sitting at the Seder and they realize that they totally forgot to clean for Pesach, and no one else seems to notice, or even care. And then they've just woken up tired.

Of course, not everyone is like that. We all know some hyper-organized individual who, no matter what time of the year you ask her, is always finished cleaning for Pesach, and makes her family eat their *chometz* in the *sukkah* all winter long and takes them on fun family trips the week before Pesach to make up for it. None of us really likes this woman, but we are all nice to her, because she organizes the carpools. And it does not help us that this woman is always really skinny, because one tends not to eat as much when he has to get dressed to go outside every time. (This is what is commonly referred to as "The Sukkos Diet.") Meanwhile, the rest of us are rushing around on *Erev* Pesach, soaking our kitchen chairs in the bathtub and sticking our heads in the oven (sometimes more than one head if it's a really big oven), while the rest of our family is standing outside trying to get the *chometz*

Cleaning House

to catch on fire. This woman reminds us all of the famous story of the grasshopper and the ant, wherein the ant cleans his home for months while the grasshopper fritters the time away working a second job and trying to figure out how to do its own taxes, when all of a sudden it's Pesach, and the grasshopper is forced to sell its *chometz*-filled home and go to a hotel, which it can't afford because there was obviously something wrong with the tax program, and the ant comes along and says, "See? You should have cleaned for Pesach when I did." So the grasshopper eats the ant, because thankfully, ants are not *chometz*. And no one likes a smart aleck. And if there's one thing that the Pesach story has taught us, it's that grasshoppers are not picky eaters.

Women and Cleaning For Pesach

The question you are probably thinking, if you're like that, is: "How come he keeps talking about cleaning in terms of *women*? Aren't men supposed to be in on this too? Why aren't *they* having these dreams?"

Well, the truth is that, while men are not having these dreams, they might be having the one in which they show up for *matzah*-baking without their shoes and socks, and the health inspector shows up and shuts the place down. But men do not generally have the cleaning dream, due to the fact that cleaning for Pesach has always fallen on the shoulders of women. This is because women see dirt better than men do. Men do not notice that a room needs to be cleaned until there is a layer of dirt thick enough to support plant life. Ask a typical man to clean the bathroom, and he will go in there with a single paper towel and a bottle of the first spray he finds — it might be Windex, it might be vegetable wash — and just spray and wipe things at random until he thinks he's been at it long enough. And you can just forget about the base of the toilet. Men are not even aware that the toilet *has* a base. Also, sometimes when men clean, the women around them (and we are not mentioning any names) keep insisting that they are actually making things dirtier. I personally have used a broom to sweep crumbs off the dining room table and onto the floor, so that I could then sweep the floor and get everything into one dustpan. My wife (whose name I will not mention) insists that this is disgusting; although I keep pointing out that I am sweeping the table with quick strokes in accordance with the five-second rule. (If you are not familiar with the five-second rule, you are definitely a woman.)

And then there are the dishes. My wife has been blessed with a slight skin condition that she says does not let her do the dishes or bathe the children. (Nothing tells the kids that Mommy loves them more than bathing them in giant dishwashing gloves.) And so, being the sympathetic husband that I am (although not sympathetic enough not to mention it in this book), I have agreed to split the chores. I come home from work *every* night and do *all* of the dishes, some of which have apparently been left there by neighbors because I can't imagine my wife eating that much, and my wife does her part by pointing out that I am not really getting anything clean. But the truth is that I'm a guy, and it does not bother me so much that the dishes are still dirty, so long as they are not taking up space in the sink.

Pesach Cleaning vs. Spring Cleaning

Once women are the ones cleaning for Pesach, the term "*chometz*" takes on a much broader meaning. Suddenly, dirt is *chometz*. Dust bunnies are *chometz*. The funny hairs at the bottom of the drain are *chometz*. Stacks of papers are *chometz*. Winter clothes at the front of the closet are *chometz*. Having the couch

Cleaning House

facing in the same direction two years in a row can be *chometz*. And you know that weird stain on your rug? The one that was there when you bought the house and that the couch was covering until about five minutes ago when the mandate came that the couch has to face the window this year to facilitate carpools? Well, that's *chometz* too.

Many men nowadays have taken it upon themselves to help their wives clean for Pesach, because we live in an enlightened society of equal treatment, meaning that men help out with the household chores and the child care, and women hold doors open for them and sometimes pay for dates. But while we men are crawling around in the attic and sorting through our children's clothing, clearly having no idea which clothes are for summer and which are for winter, and not even being entirely sure which child's clothes we are actually dealing with, once in a while we forget ourselves and blurt out that we may have heard somewhere that some of this stuff might not actually be *chometz*.

Where's our equal treatment when that happens, huh?

The problem, as many of us point out as our wives' eyes get smaller and smaller, is that women are confusing Pesach cleaning with spring cleaning. (Spring cleaning, which was invented by the *goyim*, is a way of cleaning the house in a symbolic rebirth, just as spring itself is the season of rebirth. If you can imagine such twisted *goyishe* logic.)

"Pesach Cleaning is not spring cleaning," we choke out, clearly wishing we were dead. "It's just cleaning, um, during the spring."

But the fact is that the basic *mitzvah* of cleaning for Pesach, and this can be verified by many valid sources, some of them articles written by actual women, is to clean the house to the point where it can be searched by airport security dogs, and they will come up with nothing but the ten little pieces we put out for *bedika*. (You can try walking up to airport security personnel and asking if you can borrow their dogs. But don't forget to clean your prison cell before Pesach.)

As many of these articles helpfully point out, the Talmud implies that it is possible to adequately clean your entire house after dark on the night before Pesach with a lit candle in one hand. And while that sounds an awful lot like cramming for a test, and we are tempted to point out that in those days the typical house had one room, kind of like little studio apartments, the truth is that basic Pesach cleaning in those days involved looking for food and nothing but. Imagine if they believed back then, as we do today, that dirt is *chometz*. All of their houses had dirt floors. When did the Pesach cleaning end?

Nevertheless many women believe deep down inside that America was originally discovered by some woman cleaning her dirt floor for Pesach (probably Columbus's mother). They feel that Pesach is all about showing our gratitude to Hashem by going above and beyond what we're supposed to do, just like how there are a bunch of foods we don't eat that Moshe Rabbeinu himself would think we're crazy; not that he would get the chance to say so to our faces, because we would never eat at his house on Pesach — it's *mishing*. So if we're going to thank Hashem by rearranging the furniture, then so be it.

So in the interest of keeping the peace, and seeing that this topic is not likely to be resolved in our current lifetime, I have taken the opportunity to write up an historic peace treaty, which I predict should last at least as long as any of the historic peace treaties in the Middle East:

Cleaning House

Historic Pesach Cleaning Peace Treaty

This contract hereby certifies that the man, *(name of griper)*, henceforth to be known as "the husband," and his loving wife, *(name of nagger)*, henceforth known as "the wife," being of sound mind and body, agree to abide by the following for at least the duration of time necessary to read the entire list of everything to which they are agreeing.

Article 1. The husband will pretty much go along with whatever the wife says to clean. If he honestly feels that she is asking him to clean a place where no one has ever brought *chometz* and where he is certain that no one will set foot for the entire Pesach anyway, then he can just pretend to clean it and take his chances with his wife later. In return, the wife will not ask her husband to clean out places where she herself could not imagine anyone bringing *chometz*, such as the rain gutters. Unless her husband is the type of husband who routinely goes up to "fix the shingles" on Sunday afternoons with a lawn chair and a *sefer* and some *rugelach* and no actual tools.

Article 2. The wife will remember that, although cleaning beyond the basic obligation is a good thing, yelling at her family about it turns it into a bad thing. In return, the husband will agree to stop pointing that out.

Article 3. The husband will stop *telling* his wife about how the magazine articles say that she should just clean up the *chometz* and save the dust bunnies for after Pesach. People don't like it when you flaunt it in their faces that you have time to read magazine articles. Also, no sane wife will move a breakfront just to clean the *challah* crumbs behind it, and then decide to leave the dirt there for later in the season.

Don't Yell Challah

Article 4. My wife will stop reading over my shoulder while I'm trying to write.

Moving on…

Getting Rid of Your *Chometz*

The first step in cleaning for Pesach is to use up all of the *chometz* that you already have. Actually, the first step is to stop buying it, no matter what, even though the closer you get to Pesach, the odder your meals are going to be. You may look around your kitchen and see a package of plain hot dog buns, eighteen boxes of noodles, and a sizeable jar of mustard, but to someone getting rid of *chometz*, you have what may be the makings of an interesting sandwich. I remember how one year growing up we sat down on the front porch the morning before Pesach to half a jar of pickles, two bottles of ketchup, a sample box of Cheerios with tabs cut along the sides so you could turn it into a cheapskate bowl, and some very questionable cheese. (All part of a complete breakfast.) It was a good thing I ate at the *siyum*. So the important thing is to buy your food responsibly.

Firstly, you have to ignore the sales. We all know that the supermarkets are basically going to be giving away pasta for free three weeks before Pesach. There must be something about springtime and noodles, I guess. People sometimes get so sick of noodles in the weeks before Pesach that they fantasize about not having to even think about them for an entire week. Also, you have to stay away from the price club stores, in which you push a huge shopping cart around a warehouse with no windows and lose all sense of time and say things like, "Hey, that's a good price for eight pounds of cumin!" You don't want to have to force-feed yourself eighty-six ounces of brownie mix at the last minute.

Cleaning House

But what if you're not the one buying the food? This leads us to the biggest obstacle in getting rid of food: *mishloach manos*. *Mishloach manos* is a wonderful Purim tradition that we have exactly a month before Pesach, in which we once again go beyond the call of duty and give food baskets to everyone we know, and also to everyone *they* know, and in turn we receive a truckload of food that we would never buy voluntarily, and which we now have exactly one month to get rid of.

Like halvah, for instance. What exactly is halvah? Is it *chometz*? Nobody knows. Yet many people feel compelled to include it in their *mishloach manos*, usually as part of some kind of "theme" that no one would understand if not for the helpful slip of paper they included that kindly explains that they want you to "Halvah good Purim" or "Halvah *negillah*" or "Halvah raisin celery." Whatever. They're just trying to support all of those poor halvah farmers in the Midwest. To make up for this, your *mishloach manos* theme this year should be, "Things We Bought Too Much of Because We Forgot That Pesach Is Coming." Let's hope your friends like noodles.

What to Clean

According to most authorities, the basic obligation is to clean only the places where it is likely that someone has brought some kind of *chometz* food, as well as behind the furniture where it is likely that they threw their wrappers. Of course, if you have small children, all of the rules go out the window. Children leave crumbs *everywhere*, and are constantly inventing new places to put food. On that note, don't forget to clean the salami out of the disk drive.

Also, if you have kids, you can't count on them to keep food out of the rooms that you've already cleaned. Cleaning a house

Don't Yell Challah

with kids in it is like trying to mop a floor wearing work boots. You can get every spot on the floor, but when you walk out of the room there will still be footprints. You can always try exercising strict parental discipline, by which we mean telling the kids to go play in the backyard until after Pesach. Or you can send them to the zoo with your husband to roam around aimlessly with all of the other bored fathers and big economy boxes of pretzels and overly inquisitive three-year-olds and double strollers, most of which contain at least one child with a dirty diaper that the father is not going to change because he didn't actually bring any spares, and because he already did his part by taking his kids on an outing, and because that's how the zoo smells anyway.

As far as cleaning, the key is to learn to think like your children. Rabbi Dovid Orlofsky tells a story in which a family sat down to their Seder with their air conditioner on a timer, and apparently at some point someone had stuffed a piece of bread into the air vents — a fact which the family did not discover until the timer went on and blew tiny crumbs all over their Seder table: on the *matzah*, in the salt water, everywhere.

The point of the story is that there is no way you can totally keep up with your children, so you may as well just sell your house and buy a new one, although it is probably pretty scary to spend Pesach surrounded by unopened moving boxes with no real idea of whether your kids have dropped a cookie into any of them, because they're all labeled "miscellaneous." It would be very convenient if houses came with some sort of self-clean feature, like ovens do, so that you can just turn it on and go to the zoo with your husband, and when you come back, your house will be *chometz*-free, and you will just have to replace the smoke detectors and buy new furniture and carpeting and replace the neighbors' siding.

Cleaning House

BASIC PRE-PASSOVER CLEANING CHECKLIST FOR AVERAGE HOMEOWNERS:

- ❑ House
- ❑ Car
- ❑ Place of work
- ❑ Disk drive
- ❑ Air vents
- ❑ Telephone mouthpiece holes (all)
- ❑ Cookbooks
- ❑ Parsha books
- ❑ QuickBooks

BASIC PRE-PASSOVER CLEANING CHECKLIST FOR RICH PEOPLE

- ❑ Mansion
- ❑ Summer home
- ❑ Spring and Fall homes
- ❑ Office Building
- ❑ Helicopter
- ❑ Small island
- ❑ Pockets (all)
- ❑ Pesach Hotel
- ❑ *Chometz* factory

BASIC PRE-PASSOVER CLEANING CHECKLIST FOR HOMELESS PEOPLE

- ❑ Refrigerator box
- ❑ Old refrigerator that you found when you found the box

Don't Yell Challah

- ☐ Shopping cart
- ☐ Pockets (all)
- ☐ Return cans

The Cleaning Process

The basic idea in cleaning for Pesach is to turn everything upside down and shake it, and then to cover it in contact paper just in case. The most practical method of doing this is to start at the far reaches of the house and slowly work your way toward the kitchen, so that you don't stupidly paint yourself into a corner and end up eating all of your last-minute *chometz* meals in the guest closet. Many women who would like to at least get *some* Pesach cooking done carefully leave one strange-but-not-totally-insane room to eat in, such as the basement or the garage, and then do most of their *chometz* cooking on one of those little travel burners that heat up when you plug them in, not unlike your laptop computer.

One of the most daunting things about cleaning absolutely everything you own on a deadline during tax season is the fact that, in order to get everything organized, you will first have to make a huge mess. For instance, if you look through the drawer near your telephone, which ideally should contain nothing but a few telephone books, a pad and some writing implements, you will probably find a handful of dead batteries, some random screws, a bunch of pennies, some "Box Tops for Education," a button, your old answering machine, and what appears to be a dead banana. So immediately you're going to have to start taking apart the drawer and making piles. The banana, for instance, would go in the dead-banana pile, along with the one from between the couch cushions and the one that was stuck to the ceiling fan. So

Cleaning House

if, for some reason, you have to stop in the middle of cleaning, your house will not look like it is about halfway clean, but rather like it was hit by an exceptionally well-organized tornado. This is all part of the process, though, as is illustrated in the popular cleaning-instructional book, "The Cat in the Hat Comes Back," in which the cat, who does not seem to have a name, sets out to clean a ring that he has made in someone else's bathtub, and the basic message of the book is that sometimes, if you want to clean something up, you're going to have to first invite twenty-six of your closest friends to help you smear your bathtub gunk around the lawn for a little while.

But in fact, cleaning can be fun. Okay, not as much fun as a barrel of monkeys or a hatful of tiny identical cats, but there are always little things to look forward to. Like sometimes, while you're cleaning under your bed, you're going to find something which you have torn up most of the house looking for a few months ago, and then finally caved in and bought a new one. Or maybe it's something you bought at the checkout once because you thought you needed it, even though about thirty seconds earlier you were unaware that the product had even existed, and it's been living under your bed ever since. In either case, having fun with your Pesach cleaning means that you can hold it up and proudly announce, "Hey! I've been looking for this all year!" And then add it to your Things-That-Go-Back-Under-The-Bed-When-We're-Done pile, so that you can say the same thing next year.

But the most important thing to remember in cleaning for Pesach is that you absolutely *must* have good cleaning music. You want songs that have a good beat that you can scrub along to, so cantorial music is out of the question, as that would *never* get real stains out. Ideally, you should find a tape that is somewhat Pesach-related, as it will help you get into the right frame of mind for the

Don't Yell Challah

holiday, and will probably also have some great scrubbing music. The *"Dayenu"* song, for instance, is an awesome song to scrub along to. If you have a tape that plays nothing but *"Dayenu"* over and over and over again, that is enough.

Helpful Cleaning Tips

➢ Make sure that before you begin, you have adequate cleaning supplies. This should include:
- A bunch of seemingly identical spray bottles of varying toxicity
- A vacuum cleaner
- A broom, for when the vacuum cleaner stops working
- A second broom, to push the first one out of the vacuum cleaner hose
- A big bottle of club soda
- A big bottle of Advil
- Elbow grease (any)
- Forty-seven rolls of contact paper with the goose design

➢ If you have no cleaning sprays, you can use lemon juice. Lemon juice cleans almost anything. You almost never see a dirty lemon. In fact, you can even use a lemon to clean off a bar of *soap*.

➢ You can make a homemade furniture polish using two parts olive oil and one part lemon juice, and put it into one of the spray bottles you have laying around the house that you are afraid to throw out because they still have some liquid in them, although not enough to actually come out when you squeeze the handle, and you are too afraid to pour all of those little

Cleaning House

drops into one bottle because you're not entirely sure that doing this won't cause an explosion.

- You can clean out your toaster with a standard fork, and you can get into those tiny electrical outlets with a paper clip.
- If you can get your couch out the door and over to the dry cleaners, they'll be happy to take it.
- Do not forget to clean underneath your couch cushions, because the cleaners will just keep whatever they find. Items you may find in there include: library books, magazine subscription cards, enough change to pay for the dry-cleaning on a couch, the little brush piece that came with your vacuum cleaner that you never quite figured out what to do with, the remote to your air conditioner, a mismatched sock, the pen from the phone drawer, enough crumbs to feed a hungry child in Africa, a dead banana, and that hamster that your daughter used to have.
- You can pry the computer keys off your keyboard with a flat-head screwdriver.
- You can find them under the furniture with a standard flashlight.
- You can get stains out of hard-to-reach places using your spouse's toothbrush. Just remember to put it back when you're done.
- It's always a good idea to shampoo your carpets before Pesach. If you have shag carpeting, you should also use conditioner.
- You can clean off your exercise equipment, such as your treadmill or your exercise bike, by first hanging up the huge pile of clothes you have laying on it, and then scrubbing it with your olive oil/lemon mixture. Make sure to wait until it's not slippery anymore before you put your clothes back on it. Although the

Don't Yell Challah

truth is that if you actually have *chometz* on your exercise equipment, you arguably do not even deserve to *have* exercise equipment.

- You *must* clean your vestibule. If you do not have a vestibule, or are unsure what a vestibule is, you can probably go out and rent one, and then clean it. Or you can clean someone else's.
- Do not forget to empty your vacuum cleaner bags. Contrary to popular belief, the stuff you vacuum up does not go through the cord and into the wall and back to the electric company. What would they do with it? And you very rarely hear about somebody's power going out because he's got a tissue stuck in the wires.
- Also, do not forget to sweep off the outside of your vacuum cleaner, and to vacuum the dirt off the bottom of the broom. Which of these you should do last, I do not know.

Cleaning the Kitchen

Cleaning your kitchen is tough. On the one hand, it is the most *chometz*-laden room in the house, because you eat out of it all year. On the other hand, you want to turn it into the most *chometz*-free room in the house, because you are planning on eating out of it on Pesach. So you're going to want to be even more thorough with your kitchen than you were with any other room. For instance, you should definitely scrub the ceilings; although when it comes to the rest of your house, it is generally acceptable not to clean the ceilings. Kitchen ceilings are often caked with food. I myself am guilty of sticking food onto a kitchen ceiling.

I was about seven or eight at the time, and cereal had of course gone on sale about a month or two before Pesach, so my parents

Cleaning House

ran out to the store and stocked up, out of habit, I guess. So it was basically up to me and my sister to finish a scary amount of Life Cereal, which tastes okay in moderation, but is very easy to get sick of if you're eating bowl after bowl of it for weeks. And it does not help at all that Life is the one cereal that gets soggy before you even put in the milk. You get the milk out of the fridge and then turn back to your bowl, and "Huh! It's soggy already!"

So there I was one morning, my cheeks puffed out and my mouth full of mushy cereal, that I was shoveling in like crazy because I was trying to make the bus. I was so annoyed at the situation that I took a square of cereal out of the bowl and heaved it at the ceiling. (I don't know. It made sense to me at the time.) I expected the piece of cereal to fall back down and get lost somewhere in the kitchen, so that I would just have to eat the other three hundred pieces of cereal in my bowl, but it didn't come back down. I couldn't see it on the ceiling either, because our kitchen had that weird ceiling pattern that a lot of kitchens had at the time, which was no doubt called "The Tiny Shiny Square Pattern," so I think that the cereal stuck to one of the squares and blended in. I honestly could not find it, and I was scared to mention it to my parents. There was no telling what kind of trouble I would get into for throwing a piece of cereal at the ceiling. (That also made sense to me at the time.) In retrospect, I hope my mother found it.

But you should definitely be careful about your ceilings. Even if you don't have the Tiny Shiny Square Pattern and an endless supply of cereal, there is always the portion of the ceiling above your stove, which gets all kind of splash-back and makes you wonder, as you stand on your stovetop and scrub at it, why your entire kitchen does not look like that. And then there are the mysterious handprints, which were put there by your teen-

Don't Yell Challah

aged boys, who sometimes try to enhance their Midnight Snack experience by holding contests to see who could jump up and palm the ceiling. (This may answer the question of the mysterious thumping noise coming from your bedroom floor in the middle of the night.)

Another big and complicated aspect of kitchens is the *kashering* process. *Kashering* is the process by which you make your pots and ovens and George Foreman grills fit to be used on Pesach, even though you use them for *chometz* all year long, and everything tastes like that time you burnt the gefilte fish. *Kashering* basically works by heating up the utensil with no food inside, so that instead of absorbing the taste of, say, the *kugel*, it absorbs the taste of nothing. Or, if you heat it for too long, *burnt* nothing.

There are various methods of *kashering*, based on how you normally use the utensil in question. Items that are normally heated directly, such as ovens, grills, Bunsen burners, those little travel ranges that heat up when you plug them in, and sandwich makers, are all *kashered* by letting them heat up to the point where you could basically light your *chometz* off of them, although Hashem alone knows why you want to *kasher* your sandwich maker. If these objects do not become hot enough on their own, a popular option is to use a flamethrower, because in what other scenario would a middle-aged housewife get to use a flamethrower? Of course, in the old days, they had to *kasher* their pots with two sticks or a magnifying glass. But they did have way more time on their hands, because it took them only one night to clean their homes.

As far as items that are normally used with foods, such as pots, pans, silver cups, silverware, flatware, trays, serving utensils, teakettles, and the kitchen sink, they all have to be *kashered* through immersion in boiling water. (And if you cannot for the

Cleaning House

life of you figure out how to immerse your kitchen sink in boiling water, we *will* tell you that the process involves a teakettle, and hopefully, your rabbi.)

Below are the steps necessary to clean out your kitchen, with the exception of your kitchen chairs, which we're going to assume are already soaking in the bathtub.

THE TABLE:

The procedure for the table is basically the same as for the chairs: scrub it very well, soak it in the neighbor's pool for a while, and cover it in contact paper (the table, not the pool). The contact paper will help the underside of your tablecloth remain *chometz-free*.

THE CABINETS:

Don't forget to clean the spaghetti marks off the front of your cabinets. On that note, you can also tell if spaghetti is done by tasting it.

THE REFRIGERATOR:

If you're only cleaning out the fridge once a year, then you need more help than this book can provide. But that won't stop us from trying. First, clear out everything that you're never going to eat except maybe on a bet. This includes any white foods, such as yogurt, that have started to turn green; any green foods, such as celery, that have started to turn brown; and any brown foods, such as leftover *chulent*, that have started to turn white. You should have nothing in your fridge that is not the same color it was when you bought it. Also, you should throw out everything that is growing a beard. And get your *lulav* out of there, for Pete's sake. Burn it with the *chometz* or something.

Don't Yell Challah

The next step is to take the entire fridge apart, piece by piece, using power tools if necessary, while taking care to remember which piece is which because refrigerators are *expensive*. Wash all the pieces, rinse, and repeat. If you are able to put the whole fridge back together and it still smells like feet, you can leave an open box of baking soda in there to absorb the odors. Baking soda is very good at absorbing odors, which is why they put it in toothpaste. Just make sure never to use that baking soda for cooking, but to use an entirely different box that you keep sealed, preferably in a separate house that no one lives in.

THE SINK:
If you have the kind of sink that needs contact paper, make sure it is the type of contact paper that will remain sticky even after you use the sink.

THE DISHWASHER:
We think you should get your dishwasher something nice for Pesach. Just don't call her "Dishwasher" on the card.

THE OVEN:
You should definitely use a flamethrower on this; preferably the kind that shoots out flames from over six feet away, because sticking your head in the oven is dangerous. If you have a self-cleaning oven, you can just turn it on and leave the house, because the smoke detectors will keep going off and the house will get too smoky to see anything anyway, and you don't want to be there *every* time the fire department comes by to check on it.

THE STOVE:
Stoves can get really dirty, because everything you make either splatters or spills over, and you can't just jump in and wipe it

Cleaning House

up, because it's too hot. And by the time it isn't too hot, it's crusted over. So you should definitely remove and clean all of your burners and your knobs and your round things and even the entire top of your range, but only if it is the type that comes off. My mother does not have the type of stove that comes off, but every year she tries to take it off anyway, and every year she shorts out the oven three days before the biggest food-centric holiday of the year, and every year my father has to buy a new one. You'd think that just once he'd buy one with a top that can actually come off, but the truth is that he can't afford it, because he has to keep buying new ones.

OFFICES, CUBICLES, ETC.

These are important places to clean that often get overlooked, because you are just so happy to get out of there when Pesach comes that you often forget. Also, if you work with non-Jews, you may get caught crawling around under your desk with a candle and be asked to take it outside with the smokers. And you are not really interested in standing under the overhang with a bunch of people trying to light their cigarettes off of your candle while you're carefully looking for the ten pieces of bread you hid in the ashtray. But before you brush off cleaning your cubicle, you should think about how much office cake you ate in there, and how many snacks you bought from the vending machine, and how many pieces those snacks were in from hitting the bottom of the machine. Just don't forget to warn people to duck before you start prying buttons off your keyboard.

CARS

Cleaning your car is also very important, because you spend a lot of time in there, and there's really not much to do besides eat and talk on your cell phone and maybe pick your nose. Even if you think your car looks relatively clean, just bend over sideways and twist your body around and look under the seats, and you are bound to find an endless supply of food wrappers, soda cans, and Canadian change. And if you think that's bad, take a look under your kid's car-seat. Also, some of the newer cars have millions of secret compartments, most of which are bound to contain some form of *chometz*. Our new minivan, for example, has fourteen cup holders. The van itself seats only eight people. What do they think we're doing in there?

If you don't actually have time to clean your car, you can always hire a car-cleaning service consisting of a group of *yeshiva* guys who got kicked out of their own houses for getting in the way and telling their mothers how much they do and don't have to clean and leaving handprints on the ceiling in the middle of the night. Just be forewarned that you're probably going to have to provide the cleaning supplies yourself, and that they're going to do, at best, a mediocre job, and that they're going to throw away all of your gas receipts and make off with your cans and Canadian change. And they'll probably leave footprints in the trunk.

What To Do If You Find *Chometz* On Pesach

If you find *chometz* in your possession on Pesach, the general rule is to panic and throw it down the sewer, so that it can then pass through the properties of everyone else on the block. Then you should collect yourself and go ask your rabbi, who will tell you that you should have burned it, or that it wasn't real *chometz*.

Chapter Four
The Four Major Food Groups

Buying Stock in Contact Paper

Cleaning for Pesach is all well and good, but that cannot be the whole extent of your preparations for the holiday. If it is, you may find yourself spending the entire week of Passover in an empty house — even emptier if you have the self-cleaning model — with nothing to eat but your homemade cleanser. This is why it's important to leave some time to prepare a bit of food. And maybe to buy some first.

If anybody's on top of the cleaning thing, it's the kosher supermarkets. About two months before Pesach, many of their products mysteriously vanish and are replaced by other products that look pretty much the same to the naked eye, except that their packaging is a slightly different color. Slightly different color means kosher for Passover. The shelves holding these products are carefully lined with contact paper, as are some of the checkout counters, and the products come from the factories lined with contact paper in trucks lined with contact paper, at which point they are stocked on the shelves by illegal immigrants covered in contact paper, thus assuring that the containers or boxes or cans are one hundred percent *chometz*-free, unless it turns out that the people at the box factory spilled donut sugar on the boxes. But luckily, you do not have to worry about that, because the general rule in these matters is the same principle that allows us to go on shaking the hands of total strangers and touching the doorknobs of public restrooms and doing laundry without wondering whether anyone blew their noses on any of the undershirts and just generally going about our lives without just wrapping ourselves in contact paper *every* morning, and that principal is: *If you didn't see anything disgusting happen, it never did.* Plus, you have bigger things to worry about. Like figuring out what to feed your family.

Early Pesach Products

Time was, there was not a large selection of Pesach products available. There was *matzah*, of course, and Manischewitz made *matzah* balls, because that's what they do, and Mrs. Adler made gefilte fish, which are *matzah* balls with fish in them. If people wanted a drink, there was borscht, which is basically a thick beet juice that is not made more appetizing by the fact that they put it in jars (kind of like pickle juice or the phlegm-looking stuff that comes with the fish). There was also *schav*, which was essentially green borscht. Actually, *schav* is made from sorrel leaves, which are related to spinach and beets (and quinoa). There was no quinoa juice, of course, because quinoa hadn't been brought over yet, and was still sitting around in large quantities in South America

The Four Major Food Groups

not too far from Juan Valdez, who was still putting together the Juan Valdez Haggadah.

There were also a couple of neat snacks back then. There was a potato-starch based cookie called "ladyfingers" by some shrewd marketers who decided that the image of fingers that have been worn to the bone from weeks of cleaning and cooking and *kashering* and shopping (shopping really does it to your fingers) and peeling thousands of potatoes and grinding them (the potatoes, not the fingers) into a starch and baking it into cookies was exactly what people wanted with their snack foods. But people bought it, because it was Pesach, and that was what was available. There were also macaroons, which is what happens when you try to bake a cookie without any ingredients. "Sure, we have no flour or potato starch or *matzah* meal, but we'll be fine. We've got coconuts."

People led simpler lives back then. The average housewife made most of her food from scratch, including ladyfingers. She would pluck the chickens and chop the liver and rip up the lettuce and churn the butter and milk the cows and water the fowl and make up the straw for the in-laws to sleep on and try her best not to notice that as we go on with this sentence we are creeping farther and farther back in time.

So in general, people used to buy more raw materials and fewer processed foods. They bought whole chickens and small animals from the butcher; they bought their pickles from the pickle guy; and they bought their fish on the net. The actual net, down at the docks. They spent the better part of the morning haggling with people who smelled like fishing boats, and finally they got what they felt was a great bargain, until the fishermen of course tacked on Shipping.

Don't Yell Challah

Needless to say, the world has changed drastically since then. We live in an age of instant cake mix and instant soup mix and carrots that come already peeled and cut into bite-sized pieces and softened a bit for easy chewing. We have discovered that it is far simpler, rather than having to make a cake out of eggs and water and flour and sugar, to simply make it out of eggs and water and cake mix, which contains flour and sugar in the *same box*. You can't put a price on convenience like that (besides $2.99). We have also discovered the convenience of forcing open a hermetically sealed packet of soup powder and dumping half of it on the floor and the other half into a pot of boiling water so that we can have a chemically-enhanced soup that does not actually taste like chicken, but like something we have affectionately come to know as "fake chicken." Like there are fake chickens running around on some fake farm somewhere and fighting over dehydrated corn and laying plastic eggs with toys inside and annoying the artificial beef and digging up the vegetable cubes.

So clearly, most of us cannot last an entire week without a whole slew of products to choose from.

The Whole Slew of Products to Choose From

Nowadays, when it comes to Pesach foods, you can get just about anything you would be able to purchase during the year, only it will taste a little off. Basically, there are four major foods groups. You've got your *matzah* meal, your potato products, your Passover vinegar, and of course your sugar.

MATZAH MEAL

The oldest and most well known group is that of foods made from *matzah* meal, such as certain cakes and cookies and, of

The Four Major Food Groups

course, frozen Passover pizza. The basic principle of these foods is that they contain the same ingredients that they would otherwise have during the year, only some of these ingredients were baked a few extra times. In the case of pizza, for instance, the flour is first baked into *matzah*, then broken down and kneaded again and baked into pizza dough, and then stuck in the freezer so that you can bake it again when you want to serve it. It's like having leftovers straight out of the box. Nevertheless, *matzah* meal products have proven very popular with people whose customs permit them to eat it, because, let's face it, they're not potatoes. A lot of companies are also trying to push crackers made out of *matzah* meal, secretly hoping that you won't realize that *matzos* are crackers to begin with. They've taken big crackers, broken them down into little crumbs, and then re-baked them as little crackers. The key is to figure out at what point they stopped being crunchy.

POTATO STARCH

The second of the major food groups is, of course, potatoes. The potato is an extremely versatile food, as is evidenced by the existence of the potato gun. Some products, in fact, contain more than one form of potato, such as Passover potato knishes, which consist of a mashed potato filling surrounded by dough made from potato starch. It makes you wonder why you're spending money on potatoes wrapped in more potatoes when you could do that yourself at home for cheaper. You can also buy *powdered* mashed potatoes made from potato starch, which is probably what some of these companies are putting in their knish filling, if you ask us. So it turns out that the knishes are actually potato starch wrapped in potato starch. Go figure.

There are also some companies who make a hot cereal, like farina, which they advertise as being made out of potato starch, which basically makes it powdered mashed potatoes with maple and brown sugar. And then there is potato starch pasta, which is definitely a last resort, because you're just getting over being sick of noodles, and now you're eating bad noodles made from potatoes. We can go on and on and on, but by now we're kind of sick of even *talking* about potato starch.

PASSOVER VINEGAR

The third major food group is Passover vinegar, which is a lot like regular vinegar, only it contains 100% less bread. Scientists only discovered Passover vinegar a couple of years ago, when they were actually trying to make a kosher-for-Passover disinfectant, but manufacturers have since flooded the market with new vinegar products, such as ketchup for our potato starch noodles, and, of course salsa, despite the fact that we can't eat corn chips. Unless they now make corn chips out of potatoes; I don't want to know. There's also fake mustard that contains Passover vinegar, among other things, and does not actually taste like mustard, because there's no mustard *in* it. This leads us to wonder why exactly they call it "mustard" in the first place, and not just label it as another flavor of dressing.

SUGAR

Sugar has always been one of the major food groups. This is especially true on Pesach, when there are *kitniyos* issues with high fructose corn syrup. In general, in the U.S. at least, most manufacturers opt to sweeten their foods with corn syrup rather than sugar, because of issues like color and consistency and money. (Mainly money.) This is because the government imposes high sugar tariffs, which I, for one, assumed we got rid of during

The Four Major Food Groups

the Revolutionary War (someone should check), and also because the government provides subsidies to corn farmers to keep them in the corn-growing business, so that the bulk of them don't have to resort to cutting out large portions of their fields to make mazes during tourist season. So usually when we buy something sweet we find that it is chock full of corn syrup, which is somehow magically sweet due to a process in which they let the syrup ferment in huge vats and then change its chemical structure with a good pair of tweezers and finally give up and add some honey when no one is looking. But for Passover, some companies put the extra effort into getting us some real sugar, in the form of thousands of little packets picked up over the course of the year at coffee shops, restaurants, hospitals, etc., so that we don't have to go for a whole week without things like jelly candies which melt in your mouth, and sometimes fall apart in your hand before they even get there.

One prominent company known to go out of their way to do this is Coca Cola, which, around Pesach time, makes the temporary switch to sugar, causing Coke enthusiasts (these are people who are enthusiastic about Coke to the point of medication) to rush out and drive hundreds of miles to the Jewish areas to load up their Sport Utility Vehicles with what they call, "Original Coke." (Original Coke was Kosher for Passover, apparently.) These enthusiasts meet in clubs and on the Internet to reminisce about the good ol' days when all Coke had sugar and to talk about how much they hate hate hate "Corn Syrup Coke." (I can't even tell the difference in taste at all, but they notice it enough that they obsess over one and hate the other.) They also discuss various conspiracy theories, the main one being that when Coke changed its recipe to "New Coke" back in the 1980s, they knew it would fail, but they only did so because they knew that

Don't Yell Challah

if they'd have changed it straight from "Original Coke" to "Corn Syrup Coke," the public would have forced them to switch it back. So they first came out with "New Coke," which was a flop, and then changed the recipe "back" to the way it was before, only with corn syrup instead of sugar, and people were just so happy to have their original recipe back, they just didn't care. But the Coke enthusiasts care.

Also, according to reliable sources with pickup trucks, the government is putting something addictive in Coke so that we drink a lot of it and develop cavities so that the dentists can put trackers in our teeth that tell the government exactly where we are at all hours of the day and what we are eating. "He's eating sponge cake again," they say to each other. "What is that, his fifth piece today?"

The Fact of the Matter

The fact of the matter is that, as crazy as these Coke enthusiasts sound, it is not our place, as a people, to make fun of their obsessions and their apparent abundance of spare time. We are ourselves guilty of not being able to give up the foods that we love. At least the Cokeheads are facing an eternity without their favorite drink, and are forced to act out of desperation. We can't even last a week. "Where's our mustard?! We need mustard!" *They* will stop at nothing to get at the foods that they like, while we would rather have substandard foods than give them up temporarily. While the rest of the year we would rather eat a good potato than a softish Pesach cracker. Passover has become about sitting around and complaining about how bad the food is. Instead of figuring out how to make rice out of potatoes, maybe we should just enjoy the foods that we would normally eat during the year that *aren't*

The Four Major Food Groups

chometz, such as soup and meat and salad and omelets and potato *kugel*.

Nevertheless, we insist on coming up with countless Pesach products, to the point where people say that the only thing left that is still *chometz* is actual bread. This, of course, is not true. I have personally come across kosher for Passover bread. It's made exactly like Passover cake, but without the sugar. And so we officially have nothing left. But what about the kids? When we were in school, we were taught that there were certain foods we were not allowed to eat on Pesach, such as bread and crackers and pretzels, and there were certain foods that we *could* eat, such as *matzah* and salt and ballpoint ink. But what are we going to going to tell the little kids nowadays? That we can eat pretty much eat the same foods, only they're not allowed to taste as good? Maybe we should have our first graders read the sides of the boxes and see if they can't figure out that it's just the *ingredients* that are different.

Our forefathers weren't like that. Part of the Pesach celebration is to commemorate the fact that the Jews, although the Egyptians were thoroughly defeated and mostly dead, decided to leave Egypt anyway on the word of Hashem, giving up all of the luxuries of living in what was the biggest civilization at the time, and taking along the bare minimum of food. Imagine if they would have packed along all of the Pesach products we have nowadays. How would they have kept their pizza frozen?

Of course, there are plenty of worried Jewish housewives who have announced at their engagement parties that they would adapt to their husbands' customs, and then realized that they were just blinded by the prospect of actually finding a *shidduch* and had not really thought things through as far as Pesach was concerned. Now they have quickly become Jewish mothers who express their affection through mucking around in the kitchen and are wondering how they could possibly make some sort of variety for the twenty-plus meals of Pesach before their family has potatoes coming out of their ears. But the truth is that it doesn't matter. Pesach is not about the food. Pesach is about spending time together *despite* the food.

Getting in on the Act

Regardless of how this all sounds, it is in no way a rant against the food manufacturers. They are merely individuals, Jewish or not, they have looked around with good Jewish business sense and realized that there are major issues out there that are not going to be resolved in their current lifetimes, so they might as well make some money off of them. And the fact that a lot of the food is substandard isn't their fault either, because: A. They don't have a lot to work with, and B. They are not selling, say, kosher for Passover franks-in-blankets because they have a good recipe for franks-in-blankets; they are selling it because there is a great big void in the world where franks-in-blankets should be. So really it is not their fault. But it wouldn't kill them to bring their prices down a little.

That said, I have hereby decided to get in on the act, and have come up with some ideas that are probably not already taken. If you happen to be a savvy businessman with a lot of disposable income that has somehow escaped the notice of the *yeshivas*, and you would like to throw it around a little and for some reason do not generally have a lot to do in the weeks before Pesach, I encourage you to contact me about one or more of these items, and maybe we can work something out:

The Four Major Food Groups

New Passover Product Ideas

18-Minute Beer™

From the moment the barley comes into contact with water until the final pasteurization, the entire brewing process for this fine product takes just under 18 minutes. Though not entirely drinkable, it is guaranteed to get your friends to come over to your house for yom tov.

Potato Seasoning®

This perfect blend of only the finest salts and peppers is a perfect compliment to any form of the potato, be it baked, fried, mashed, or fired from a potato gun. No more will potatoes be boring. There's nothing less boring about a potato than having it covered in our delicious seasoning, crashing through your living room window. (Also available in Maple and Brown Sugar.)

Powdered Salt Water ©

Just add water.

Matzah-Shaped Cookie Cutters ☺

Also available in potato shape and egg shape.

Pre-made *Matzah-Marror* Sandwiches ⊛

For the train. Also can be enjoyed at zoos, especially if you try feeding them to the animals.

Camouflaged *Afikoman* Bags 👁

These are available in "bookshelf," "fish tank," and "pile of Haggados."

Don't Yell Challah

Matzah-Print Contact Paper

> This product is a nice change from the regular, boring contact paper that we usually use to line our kitchen counters, and is a way to get a toe-hold in the market of the "matzah-print" industry, which now includes matzah notebooks, bibs, yarmulkes, and a little stuffed baker guy who sings, kind of like that annoying singing mounted fish that everyone bought back when it came out, and then got sick of because it only played those same two infernal sound bites, and promptly packed them away in their basements, where they occasionally spring to life and scare the webbing out of curious spiders. On the other hand, this contact paper is sure to freak out people who are careful about gebruktz.

"I Can't Believe It's Not *Chometz*" Spread

> Taste it— you won't believe it's not chometz.

Gebrux-Lax

> For those who feel that saliva may make things gebruktz, this product is guaranteed to wash out your entire system in less than 18 minutes. This is especially effective on 18-Minute Beer.

Matzah Watched From The Time Of Planting

> Sure to be popular with people who enjoy going beyond the letter of the law, this matzah is watched from the time the grain is planted to make sure it never comes into contact with water. (NOTE TO INVESTORS: This may not be feasible, as the last time we tried this, we couldn't get anything to grow.)

Other Things to Buy

Once you buy food, you're probably going to need something to put it on; ergo you should get yourself some plates and pots and

The Four Major Food Groups

pans and George Foreman grills, and maybe even a tablecloth, if you're of the female gender. Most of these items will have to be *toiveled* (or dipped) in a *mikvah* (or lake) in order to make them Jewish, with the possible exception of the tablecloth.

Official *Toiveling* Primer:

1. Load up all of your new dishes, flatware, etc and drive them over to the local *mikvah* and stand in the longest line that you see. If everyone in the line is holding a small hotel soap and has a towel over his shoulder, you may be at the wrong kind of *mikvah*. It is always good to ask. Try looking for a line consisting of a bunch of people struggling under the weight of awkwardly shaped boxes, punctuated by a couple of frustrated people swinging around a single coffee mug. If you are doing your *toiveling* at a lake, it's pretty silly to stand in line. It's a *lake*. Go directly to Step 2.

2. Using a sharp object, and with all of the people in line behind you giving you dirty looks, open all of your packaging and take out what you need *toiveled*. If all of your sharp objects are still in their packaging and that's why you're there in the first place, ask the person in front of you if you can use one of his. Or you can take a deep breath and reach way into the *mikvah* and pick up a fork that someone dropped in.

3. Using your sharp object or a fingernail, scrape the stickers off every single dish, spoon, etc. No one knows why the anti-Semites at the packing plant feel they have to put stickers on every last plate, especially since they don't sell them individually anyway, but you can be assured that they are there.

Don't Yell Challah

4. Say the proper blessing and start dipping, making sure to hold each item loosely enough so that the water can touch every part of it, but not loosely enough that it will end up at the bottom of the lake. The bottoms of most *mikvahs* are lined with brand new flatware, kind of like the pennies in the mall fountain, and every once in a while they scoop them all up and use the proceeds to pay the water bill. Grills, however, are not as much of a problem, so long as you can tether the wire to the person behind you while you submerge the rest of it.

5. Gather up whatever's left of your stuff and put them back into the boxes for easy transport. On the way to the car the plates will soak through the boxes and come crashing to the ground, so you probably should have stood in the line with the towels.

6. Go home and use plastic plates. After all, that's what they did in the desert.

The Alternative

There are a lot of people out there, such as your neighbors who claim they have no money, who would rather not bother with cooking and figuring out which products to buy and losing their silverware and breaking their dishes. These people opt, instead, to leave their houses and spend Pesach at exotic locations, thereby carrying on the tradition of our forefathers, who left their homes and headed for the desert, the only difference being that some of these exotic locations have workout rooms, whereas the desert was just a big treadmill.

The main feature that these places advertise is the food, which is under the strict supervision of a major prominent rabbi, whose

The Four Major Food Groups

picture is often in the ad so you can see just *how* prominent. The only problem is that while many of these rabbis keep an *eye* on the food *preparations*, when it comes to actually serving the food, they regretfully cannot be there, because they are at home spending *yom tov* with their families, because there has yet to be a rabbi's wife who would *ever* let someone else do her cooking. So a lot of times, the rabbi just hires a stand-in *mashgiach* in the form of a *yeshiva* student, and not necessarily the kind who wants to grow up to become a rabbi. In fact, many times these guys cannot answer simple questions on their own, such as whether or not quinoa is *kitniyos*.

This is not really a problem, though. The truth of the matter is that all of the food is already on site and the kitchen was already blowtorched and the food was already cooked, and basically all the kid has to do is keep an *eye* on the kitchen personnel and make sure that the blue stuff stays in the blue kitchen, and the red stuff stays in the red kitchen, and that none of the kitchen staff realizes how the Passover food doesn't quite taste right and decides to walk in one day with a ham sandwich, both because of the ham, and because of the sandwich.

In fact, I myself spent almost two years as a morning *mashgiach* in a nursing home, which shall remain nameless because I don't want an angry phone call asking me why people are suddenly yanking out their grandparents. My job was to come in late every morning and crawl around on the busy kitchen floor in a long white doctor's coat and blow out all of the pilot lights (*everything* there seemed to have a pilot light, including the walk-in freezer), and then make several abortive attempts to relight them with the kitchen staff breathing down my neck and rolling their eyes about how I had to interrupt their cooking routines just to make sure

Don't Yell Challah

everything was kosher. And if you think *they* were frustrated, you should have seen the laundry manager.

I would then spend the rest of the morning walking back and forth from kitchen to kitchen, pretending to be interested in what everyone was doing, but really just training my eyes for an out-of-place pot or pan, and for people forgetting to wear their gloves. If I found something out of place, my job was to confiscate it and bring it to the tiny rabbi's office (the office was tiny, the rabbi was regular) and add it to the pile, and the rabbi would deal with it when he had time, which he never did, as is evidenced by the fact that he couldn't even be there in the mornings. I think that he was actually teaching a class then, because when I called to tell him what happened or to ask him questions, he kept interrupting me to tell people to sit down. Or maybe he was a flight attendant. But I assume that most of the pans are still there, crowding the office. The worst was when I had to confiscate an entire serving cart.

So I can pretty much tell you, from experience, that the food at most of these hotels is probably okay. But I would definitely say that your best bet, if you want a good meal but don't want to cook for it, is to eat at the rabbi's house. Let *him* do the shopping. Or else he should just send his *yeshiva* guy.

Chapter Five
The *Matzah* Factory

A Hands-Off Education

Of all the steps of Pesach preparation, *matzah* baking is definitely one of the most interesting, at least in terms of class trips. It's definitely more interesting than the class trips to clean the *rebbi*'s car. "This will teach you about the cleaning process." Sure. Whatever.

I remember my very first trip to the *matzah* bakery. I was five years old at the time, and my *rebbi* had decided it would be a good idea to take the entire kindergarten class on a field trip. In retrospect, he obviously hadn't thought things through. There was no way that the management was going to allow thirty curious five-year-old boys to wander around a live *matzah* bakery. Instead, they made us all stand out near the front, behind a counter that was about elbow height — to our *rebbi*. For the rest of us, it was way over our heads. And so our *rebbi* dutifully held each of us up, one at a time, to see what was going on behind the counter.

Don't Yell Challah

We each got about three seconds to take it all in, as the *rebbi* was slowly getting exhausted from lifting thirty kids. When it was my turn, I caught a brief glimpse of some old guy washing a big metal mixing bowl at the sink. I cannot tell you how that experience has changed my perspective on *matzah*-baking forever. But we did stop for pizza on the way back.

The first time that I went to a *matzah* bakery where I actually knew what was going on, I was well into my teenage years, and, of course, it was another class trip. This time, they let our *rebbi* lead us through the different rooms so that we could see exactly what was going on, and so the *rebbi* could point out that it was going exactly how we had learnt in class that it should. Big mixing guy, little old ladies with rolling pins, middle-aged man in sweats standing in front of an oven, eighteen minute shifts, old man at the sink in the other room washing the mixing bowls. Nevertheless, the management still would not let us actually assist in the baking process, because you don't want to give a group of teenagers access to a two-thousand degree oven, a bunch of wooden sticks of various sizes, and a paint roller with nails sticking out of it. What we learned that day was that you never really grow up, you just get taller. We also learned that if you ask for free samples at the end of the tour, they will actually laugh you out of the building. At least that's better than what they do if you ask that at the U.S. Mint.

The Twelve-Step Program for Baking *Matzah*

STEP 1: Begin a Twelve-Step Program.

So you want to give up *chometz*. Congratulations! *Chometz* is evil! *Chometz* is the *yetzer hara*! We're going to need to get you some *shmura matzah*.

The Matzah Factory

The first step toward making *matzah* is harvesting the wheat. Actually, the first step is growing the wheat, but wheat growing is not what makes the *matzah* process interesting. The wheat is cut with big combine harvesters that look like the kind of truck that would get pulled over if you took is out onto the highway, because it has huge spinning blades on the front that you might be tempted to use in traffic situations. A trained rabbi has to come in and watch the harvesting process to make sure they don't do it on a rainy day and mess everyone up to begin with.

Under supervision of the rabbi, the wheat undergoes a long and probably tedious process wherein it is transformed from big stalks into fine flour using *kabbalah*. The transformation process is not covered at all in the *matzah* bakery tour, although it may involve something called a millstone, which is kind of a cross between a steamroller and a CD player. The flour is then dry cleaned (the dry-cleaners don't understand why we give them all that flour, but are thrilled for the business) and sealed up into large pillowcases.

STEP 2: Get the Flour To The Bakery.

This is accomplished via a clean, blowtorched truck. (If no such trucks are available, they use minivans.) The trucker must drive very cautiously throughout the trip, because he knows that if he gets into an accident, he will lower the visibility for miles around. Also, he will disqualify all of the flour, and totally cover the rabbi sitting in the back of the truck.

STEP 3: Place the Flour into Solitary Confinement.

The flour is placed into a small, cool, dry, well-ventilated, well-insulated little closet at the side of the bakery along with a guy with big white handprints on his pants. The door to this closet is kept closed at all times, and the flour can only leave the room in precisely-measured amounts through a tiny window when a big, muscle-bound mixer person gives the code phrase. The flour guy is fed dry foods through the little window, and is let out after Pesach when the Rabbi buys back the factory.

STEP 4: Put Together All of the Ingredients.

Starting a timer for eighteen minutes, the mixer person grabs a mixing bowl, knocks on the little window and gives the code phrase, (The code phrase ranges from "Nu?" to "The sun shines on the shop sign.") and a hand pops out and pours a scoop of flour into the bowl. He then brings the bowl to another little window and a hand pops out with a cup of water. (When it comes to making *matzos*, anonymity is key, and so the flour and water guys can never meet, or the universe will become *chometz*.)

The mixer person puts the entire bowl on a pedestal (both physically and spiritually) and goes into a mixing frenzy, mixing and patting and swirling and punching and kicking and screaming for a solid twenty seconds until the bowl contains nothing but a perfect mound of dough. It is generally a good idea to have him remove his watch first.

STEP 5: Keep the Dough Moving.

The mixer person hands the dough off to another guy whose job it is to play around with it until he gets the signal from the old ladies with the rollers. If the dough stops moving, it may become *chometz*, so this guy has to really keep at it, rolling it and kneading

The Matzah Factory

it and making funny animal shapes and, "Hey, look! I made a *challah*!"

Never yell "*Challah!*" in a crowded *matzah* bakery.

In the meantime, the mixer guy grabs himself another bowl, knocks on Little Window #1, and yells, "Nu?" You can't have the flour and water guys in their little closets taking seventeen-minute naps.

STEP 6: Roll, Roll, Roll Your Dough

The dough is broken up and distributed to the Rollers, usually a bunch of old *bubbies* standing around a table with rolling pins. As it turns out, only a certified bubby with years of experience can roll a small piece of dough with a stick and have it come out perfectly round. I've tried rolling some dough once, and the shape I came up with doesn't even have a name. So there's a lot of respect there. This is the one job where you can actually put "mother of ten" on your resume and be taken seriously.

It's difficult to say exactly how the *bubby*-hiring process works. Chances are they all know and recommend each other, their being *bubbies* and all. Or maybe the bakery puts ads in the paper:

> **BUBBY WANTED**
> Must have experience working long hours,
> Spending all day on her feet,
> And cleaning the same room every twenty minutes.
> No Zeidies need apply.

Personally, I picture a clot of *bubbies* standing out in front of Home Depot in the morning, waiting for a day's work, and the

Don't Yell Challah

owner of the *matzah* bakery coming by in a pick-up truck: "All right, I'm gonna need eight *bubbies*!"

Nevertheless, the *bubbies* add to the hominess of the *matzah* bakery, providing each other with support and encouragement, and making *shidduchim* during the break time. Sometimes they even try to make *shidduchim* for each other:

"How about the gentleman washing the mixing bowls over by the sink? You already know he does dishes."

"I don't know. I'd really prefer someone who's still in *yeshiva*. What do his kids do for a living?"

STEP 7: Pat it, Prick it, and Mark it With Braille

When the Bubbies are finished rolling, someone takes the dough from them, and their supervisor stops fooling around with the next batch of dough and cuts it up and passes it around. He's handed a fresh piece of dough by the mixer guy, who grabs another bowl and interrupts the flour guy's coughing fit to say "Nu?"

The flattened dough, meanwhile, is given to a Pricker, who wields the paint roller with the nails sticking out of it, and makes lots of tiny holes in the *matzah* so that it doesn't swell up in the oven like a bag of popcorn. That paint roller has got to be murder to clean.

STEP 8: Prep the Matzos. Stat!

Another person stands next to the Pricker and snatches the discs out from under him and throws them over a huge pole, kind of like a twelve-foot shish kabob. He then picks up the pole and

The Matzah Factory

runs pell-mell into the baking room. This Prepper (Preppie?) must have a unique combination of guts and recklessness that will allow him to continuously stick his hands under the paint roller and run across a crowded room with a twelve-foot pole.

STEP 9: Bake at Two Thousand Degrees for Twenty Seconds.

The Preppie (Prepper?) hands the pole to a middle aged man in sweats, and then runs off to get another pole, in part because the baking room itself is about three-hundred degrees Fahrenheit. The Baker slides the *matzos* into the oven, laying them flat, and then smears himself in another layer of suntan lotion before grabbing a huge shovel and taking out the *matzos*. By then the guy with the pole is back, and he has to move quickly because the Pricker is waiting on him because the *bubbies* are almost finished rolling and another batch is ready for them in the shape of a *korban* Pesach because the Mixer is working on another batch and the flour guy is on the phone with the trucker who is driving slowly because he doesn't want to cover the rabbi in the back of the truck. So all of this has to be a delicately timed process, in order to get as many batches as possible done in eighteen minutes.

To help keep everyone's focus on the importance of what they are doing, the bakery workers periodically shout out, "*L'shem matzas mitzvah!*" meaning "For the sake of the *matzah* that will be used for the *mitzvah!*" This is very important. At a machine *matzah* factory, the machine must periodically spit out a little slip of paper that says it too. On some days the Mixer guy uses it as his secret code phrase, but then everyone else starts yelling it, and the flour guy gets confused.

Don't Yell Challah

STEP 10: Check for Imperfections.

Even when you're dealing with the most skilled professionals, mistakes do happen. It is the job of the quality control department to inspect every *matzah* for bubbles and folds, and probably to taste a few at random. If any imperfections are found, they are disposed of, and the responsible party is locked in the flour closet the next year.

STEP 11: Package the *Matzos*. In packages.

The *matzos* are weighed and placed into hatboxes, which are imprinted with the name of the *matzah* bakery, often in long pseudo-Hebraic words without any pronunciation cues. They are then sold by the pound, with one pound being equal to about eight whole *matzos*, or 135 shards (more often 135 shards), and are sold for the price of an *esrog*. But this is not really a lot of money when you consider how much sweat and tears go into them.

STEP 12: Rinse. Repeat.

When the eighteen-minute buzzer sounds, everything is cleaned and wiped and sanded and washed and replaced, and there is a major line at the coffee machine. Two minutes later, the cycle starts over, and so on, until the bus comes to take the *bubbies* back to the retirement village.

Round Versus Square *Matzah*: Which is Better?

Originally, all *matzos* were round. The round shape symbolized the singularity of Hashem and the unity of the Jewish people and

The Matzah Factory

death and mourning and the circle of life and the Four Seasons Hotel and the fact that we seem to be going in circles. If you would have gone back to the time of Mordechai and Esther and shown them a square *matzah*, they would have thrown you out, in part because they were fasting.

But then one day, in the late 1800s, the machine *matzah* was invented in Austria by Irving and Ida Machine, who discovered that, by simply letting twin rollers press the dough and slide it into a mechanical oven, they could lay off thousands of *bubbies*, thus causing a significant decline in the price of *matzah*, to the point where they could give it away for free if you bought fifty dollars worth of groceries. (In those days, fifty dollars bought enough groceries for the whole Austria.)

But this did not sit well with a lot of the rabbis, not to mention the Rolling Bubbies Union. They said that tradition maintained that *matzos* should be made the way our forefathers did — on our backs, in the desert. Or at least it should be made by hand, like the rest of our forefathers, besides for Mordechai and Esther that one year. They also said that there was no way that the machine was going to get cleaned properly, despite the fact that it tended to spontaneously burst into flames at random intervals. And many of the *bubbies* depended on their *matzah*-baking income, because they were illegal immigrants who came into the country to escape persecution by working in a basement with no windows and hiding from immigration.

Nowadays, however, there have been a lot of technological improvements, to the point where machine *matzah* is sometimes more reliable than hand *matzah*, and the machines do not explode nearly as often. But baking hand *matzah* is definitely more interesting to watch. There are very few schools that make it a

Don't Yell Challah

point to take the children to the machine *matzah* factory to watch a guy press a button in the morning.

As for which one tastes better, we would definitely have to go with hand *matzah*, as machine *matzah* tends to be kind of bland. Apparently, the taste of the *matzah* comes from all of the hands involved.

Making *Matzah* at Home

You can also make *matzah* from the safety of your very own home, provided you make sure to get rid of it before Pesach comes. Because there's no way you're going to do it right. For one thing, you're already preheating your oven on "self-clean."

YOU WILL NEED:

- ❑ 3 parts flour
- ❑ 1 part water
- ❑ 2 measuring cups
- ❑ 1 mixing bowl and pedestal. If you have no pedestal to hold the bowl in place, you may end up with both hands in the bowl, chasing it around on the counter.
- ❑ 1 rolling pin
- ❑ 1 couple of forks, for pricking purposes
- ❑ 1 baking sheet
- ❑ 1 oven
- ❑ 1 fire extinguisher

If you are a child, you will need your parents' permission. If not, you will need to make sure your significant other is out of the house.

The Matzah Factory

BAKING INSTRUCTIONS:

The baking instructions are self-explanatory, provided you've been paying attention. If you haven't, then you're definitely off to a great start. The key is figuring out at what baking temperature to set the oven so that you can keep the entire process under eighteen minutes. To do this, you can use a simple mathematical formula:

It usually takes about twenty to thirty seconds to bake a *matzah* in a two thousand degree oven. How long will it take to bake a *matzah* in a four hundred-fifty degree oven if you have to pick up your spouse from the train at five-thirty? Logic tells us it will take about two minutes, so it's not a big deal, unless you consider that the real world doesn't work that way. If you're supposed to bake a cake for an hour at three-fifty, you can't just decide to bake it for a half-hour at seven hundred. When I tried this recipe, it took me sixteen minutes just to bake the *matzos*, and my wife wanted to know why the house smelled funny. So you'll just have to play it by ear.

Chapter Six

Recipes for Disaster

Ice Cubes

Source: The Fat-Free Cholesterol-Free Vegetarian Cookbook For Chassidishe-Yekke Lubavitchers with Allergies

YOU WILL NEED:
- 2-3 cups Kosher-for-Passover homogenized filtered spring water
- 1 working freezer
- 2 ice cube trays, or 28 shot glasses and a roomy freezer

INSTRUCTIONS:

In a clean room, filter water through cheesecloth or an unused sock to remove all unwanted organisms. Dole out water into ice cube trays or shot glasses in equal amounts using a medicine dropper. Carefully hold tray perfectly level with both hands, and try to open the freezer with your face. Set tray down and open freezer normally. Turn around to pick up tray, while freezer door

Don't Yell Challah

closes behind you. Set tray back down and open the door again, this time keeping your head in the path of the freezer door. Pick up the tray again and brace for impact. If you still haven't spilled any of the water, carefully place tray on freezer door and swing shut. Allow 6 hours to cool. Serve with drinks or in really hot soup.

Homemade Gefilte Fish

Source: "Do You Smell Fish?" A Pareve Cookbook

YOU WILL NEED:

- ❑ 12 Pounds of boneless ground fish
- ❑ 1 carrot
- ❑ Salt, sugar, pepper, onions, eggs to taste

INSTRUCTIONS:

In a clean room, set up about a dozen scented candles and begin thawing your fish. Almost any type of random dead fish will do, although the classy approach is not to use tuna. Fish can be purchased at a local fish store, unless your local fish store has closed down because the proprietor realized that people really only come in twice a year. If that is the case, you can always go fishing on your own, thereby providing yourself with an excuse to get out of the house during Pesach cleaning. Or you can just try the local pet shop. Just don't tell them what you're doing with your purchases.

PET STORE GUY: "This is a lovely fish, but it's very expensive to maintain. You're going to need an aquarium, a filter, a heater, a

Recipes for Disaster

thermometer, a lifesaver, and a little fake treasure chest that blows bubbles *every* eight seconds."

YOU: "That's nice. Do you have one that's maybe twelve pounds?"

Once you get home, cut the fish open and take out the bones, but for heaven's sake don't throw them away! You're going to need them to make fish broth! In fact, get the broth started right now, before you forget. Just add water to your bones, and then add onions, salt, pepper, a bay leaf (why not?), and, of course, your carrot. Federal law requires that *every* piece of gefilte fish have a small sliver of carrot on top, to make sure that guests and *kiddush* attendees don't mistake them for cookies. The carrots are definitely not there to make the fish look pretty, because there's really only so much you can do with a small orange circle on a gray background. And they're not there to improve the taste either, or else we would positively *drown* it in carrots. But we don't. We drown it in beets. So maybe we should put a little sliver of beet on the fish.

While your broth is boiling, but hopefully not boiling over, figure out how to grind up your fish so that it looks like something you would pull out of your drain, and then add onions, salt, pepper, a bay leaf, (why not?) and *eggs*. Mix the ingredients by hand in the same manner as the Mixer Guy over at the *matzah* bakery, and if everything goes well it should not take you more than about twenty seconds. Being careful not to slip, carry your fish over to the stove and drop it into the broth in whatever shape you wish it to be. Most people make fish balls or big loaves, but if you want to confuse the kids, you can shape it into an actual fish, using a carrot as the *eye*.

Don't Yell Challah

Allow fish to cook for one hour, or until it's done. (No, I don't know how to tell when it's done. Taste it, I guess.) Remove the bones, as well as the bay leaves, if you can find them. Place the fish in the fridge and allow it to cool. Feeds one army.

Square Matzah Balls

Source: 101 Matzah Ball Recipes for All Occasions

YOU WILL NEED:

- ❑ 1 box square *matzah*
- ❑ Some eggs
- ❑ 3 pinches salt
- ❑ ½ pinch pepper
- ❑ Water or seltzer or Passover Coke

INSTRUCTIONS:

In a clean room, cram as many *matzos* as you can into a blender or food processor or cleanish garbage disposal and turn it on. Go out and run some errands, and you will come back to find that the *matzah* has turned into a fine *matzah* meal that will spill out onto your counter when you force the lid off the blender. Gather up your remaining *matzah* meal and mix it with your eggs, salt, pepper, and water or soda. Spoon this mixture into an ice cube tray and leave it in the freezer next to your ice cubes (see ice cube recipe), making sure you remember which is which. When *matzah* cubes are sufficiently frozen, twist tray over a pot of boiling water so that they PLOP in and splash excess water into your fish broth. Wait until *matzah* balls expand and most probably lose their

Recipes for Disaster

cube shape, and spoon them into an already-made soup. (Maybe we should have put the soup recipe first.)

If you do not eat *gebruktz*, simply leave out the *matzah* meal.

Chicken Soup

Source: The Artscroll Hebrew-English Cookbook Zichron Bubbie

YOU WILL NEED:

- ❑ 1 dead bird, usually chicken
- ❑ A LOT of water
- ❑ 4 carrots
- ❑ 2 stalks celery
- ❑ 3 cups salt
- ❑ 1 cup bay leaves
- ❑ 1 pepper, black
- ❑ 1 or more onions
- ❑ Random Spring vegetables

INSTRUCTIONS:

In a clean room, boil one humongous pot of water and go about cleaning your chicken. If you are unable to get hold of a chicken, almost any bird will do.

YOU: "I'm looking for a domesticated bird that weighs about three pounds."

Don't Yell Challah

PET STORE GUY: "Hey, aren't you the guy who bought three hundred goldfish this morning?"

When your bird is reasonably clean, put away your soap and your toothbrush and carefully PLOP it into the boiling water. (Allow one week to boil.) Peel and circumcise carrots, and test them to make sure they are fresh. (A carrot that you can tie into a knot is not fresh.) But even if it's not fresh, no one will know; it's *soup*, after all. Chop up carrots, celery, onions, and random vegetables and add them to the soup. Also add salt and pepper and bay leaves while you're at it. Eventually, the water will turn beige, which means that the soup is ready, or else it means that you didn't do a good job cleaning the chicken. When the soup is done, make room in your fridge, taking out shelves if necessary, and refrigerate overnight. In the morning, carefully scrape off the thin layer of fat and crud that congealed at the top and find another recipe that calls for it. Reheat your soup and PLOP in your *matzah* balls.

Serves 80, 12 of whom will want no carrots, 18 of whom will want *only* carrots, 20 of whom will want clear soup, 10 of whom will want to add either salt or pepper, 5 of whom will want only the spring vegetables and no actual water, 10 of whom will want everyone else's *matzah* balls, and 5 of whom will specifically gnaw on the chicken bones like you're not feeding them enough.

Recipes for Disaster

Kitniyos Salad

Source: "BEANS!!!"
The Cookbook for Sefardim

YOU WILL NEED:

- ❑ 3 bean salad (optional)
- ❑ 1 cup chick peas (optional)
- ❑ 1 cup corn or 2 ears corn or ½ can of corn (optional)
- ❑ 1 cup snow peas (optional)
- ❑ 1 cup jelly beans (optional)
- ❑ 1 cup linseed oil (optional)
- ❑ 1 cup groats (optional)
- ❑ 1 cup honey mustard dressing with added millet (optional)

INSTRUCTIONS:

In a clean room (optional), chop beans into small pieces with a very good knife, and place them into a large fancy bowl or vase. Open windows and serve.

(NOTE: Before serving, make sure that everyone else at the table is Sefardi, so that no one has to awkwardly stammer, "Um, I don't eat *kitniyos* this week," thus causing you to apologize and quickly scoop them off the table, thereby disappointing the rest of your guests to the point where some of them will actually storm off in disgust. Instead, you must find a way to nonchalantly work it into a conversation beforehand. For example, you can say: "You're not one of those crazy paranoid Ashkenazim, are you?" Or, "Speaking of awkward silences, when was the last time you ate beans?" Or else you can just give them the quiz at the end of Chapter 1. Either way, you should not actually tempt Ashkenazim with this dish. You may, however, casually talk about your salad in

Don't Yell Challah

every single conversation you have with your Ashkenazi neighbors that week.)

⁂

Passover Chicken with Apricots, Olives, Onions, Parsley and Salt

Source: The Maxwell House Cookbook

YOU WILL NEED:

- ❏ Passover chicken
- ❏ Apricots
- ❏ Olives
- ❏ Onions
- ❏ Parsley
- ❏ Salt
- ❏ Bay leaf

INSTRUCTIONS:

In a clean room, think about how painfully obvious some recipes are when you look at their names. Reflect on how thoughtful the people who came up with these recipes were for giving us hints like that, rather than just naming the recipes after themselves, i.e., Chicken Alfredo, General Tso's Chicken, Herb Chicken, Fried Chicken (as in Avraham Fried), and Chicken Kiev, which was invented by the entire town of Kiev one crazy Friday afternoon. Those recipes give absolutely no clue as to what's in them, and you have to read through the entire recipe in order to realize that you don't have half the ingredients. Whereas recipes like this one, which list everything right in the title, give you the

Recipes for Disaster

ability to tell at a glance whether it sounds like something you'd want to eat, as well as telling you right off the bat that if you don't have apricots or onions or salt, then you shouldn't even bother.

Next, clean your chicken, using a bottle brush if necessary, and put it in a pan with the rest of the ingredients, some of them cut, some of them pitted, and some of them sprinkled. Bake until the inside of the chicken is no longer red. (You can easily determine this if you have psychic powers. Or else you have to go on guesswork.)

Serves however many members of your family trust your guesswork.

Green Eggs and Lamb

Source: "Oh Say Can You Cook?"
By Dr. Seuss, F.S. (Food Scientist)

YOU WILL NEED:
- 1 lamb
- 3 dozen eggs, aged
- Passover food coloring (3 parts blue to 2 parts yellow)
- 1 mouse
- 1 house
- 1 train
- 1 bucket rain
- Oil, for frying
- 1 zizzer zazzer zuzz (fresh)

Don't Yell Challah

INSTRUCTIONS:

In a clean room, separate one lamb shank and one egg for use on your Seder plate. Braise the remainder of the lamb, with a braiser, apparently, or simply sauté in a greased frying pan. In a separate bowl, break open the remainder of your eggs and add desired amount of rain for texture. Scramble. In yet another very small bowl or bottle cap, mix 3 drops of blue food coloring and 2 drops of yellow with a toothpick, and add to eggs. (Or you can just dump in three bottles of blue and two of yellow. Or you can just use green food coloring in the first place, if you are the type of person who needs everything pre-made for them.) Repeat this process until eggs are the desired shade of green. Eggs should be more of a pistachio ice cream green and less of a military camouflage or a congealed pea soup green. Pour eggs into pan and fry until you think it may be time to flip them over. Fry them some more and flip them again; fry them some more and flip them again; fry them some more, scrape them off the bottom of the pan, and open your windows.

Serves all of your friends and loved ones, provided you are willing to chase them around town with a plate balanced over your head to get them to try it. Makes for a fun yet suspenseful Passover entrée: Will they eat it topped with *chrain*? Will they eat it in the rain? Will they eat it under an umbrella? Will they die of salmonella?

Recipes for Disaster

Pesach Cholent

Source: Cooking With Nothing – A Passover Cookbook

YOU WILL NEED:

- ❏ 1 meat
- ❏ 1 truckload potatoes, peeled
- ❏ Last year's leftover *cholent*
- ❏ Odds and Ends, to taste

INSTRUCTIONS:

In a clean room, put your meat into the biggest pot you own that is not already occupied by either a fish or a chicken. Then get started on your potatoes. The key to making Pesach *cholent* is to remember that your potatoes are actually standing in for:

Your beans, the exact names of which you don't know because they normally come in a big bag labeled "*cholent* mix."

Your barley, which you definitely cannot use, because letting barley sit on a stove overnight in a pot of *cholent* is actually hands-down the most *chometz* way to eat barley (not counting the *sotah*-method, in which the person eating it actually expands and becomes *chometz*).

Your beer, which is added mainly by newly married guys trying to show their wives that they can make something other than grilled cheese.

Your rice, which is added, mainly by women, to absorb all of the beer.

The potatoes that you *usually* put in the *cholent*. You can't forget those.

Don't Yell Challah

Thus you're going to have to use a lot of potatoes, and fast. The basic idea is to make them into a lot of different consistencies, so that they can stand in for all of the various items. Thus, you can slice a few and dice a few and grate a bunch and puree the rest. That way, you get one big mush that somewhat resembles a regular *cholent*, although you can't help but feel that it more closely resembles what would happen if the truckload of potatoes got into an accident with a cement mixer. To distract from this, you can add your leftovers and your odds/ends, although that will probably not help. It is recommended that the person who makes the *cholent* just hangs back and does not actually eat it.

Chocolate-Covered Matzah

Source: The "I'll Diet After Yom Tov" Cookbook

YOU WILL NEED:

- Flour
- Water
- Melted chocolate
- Fondue set

INSTRUCTIONS:

Cover a clean room floor to ceiling with a *serious* drop cloth. Load up fondue set with chocolate, or else you can make your own chocolate using baking cocoa, margarine, and enough sugar to put a small animal into a coma. In a separate bowl, mix your *matzah* ingredients, roll into discs or rhomboids or whatever, and bake. Wearing a smock or a *kittel*, dip one end of your *matzah* at a time into the chocolate sauce, taking care not to drop the

Recipes for Disaster

whole *matzah* into the pot. Allow *matzos* to cool. Makes for an exciting albeit slightly dangerous snack. Top your *matzah* with jelly or cream cheese or horseradish.

~~~~

Potato Gun

Source: 613 Things to do With a Potato

YOU WILL NEED:

- Permission from your parents, even if they live down in Florida or are dead.
- 1 absentee spouse
- 1 friend or child who is willing to stand back at a safe distance and hold a phone on which he or she has already dialed the whole number for Hatzalah except for the last digit.
- A 4-foot section of 2-inch PVC pipe (PVC is the really hard plastic pipe you have that noisily carries water from your basement to your upstairs bathroom and back via the wall between your dining room and your kitchen.)
- A 2-foot section of 4-inch PVC pipe
- A 4-inch-to-2-inch reducer (In English, a funnel.)
- A 4 inch sewer plug (new)
- An electric barbeque starter
- Screws
- Epoxy
- Hair spray

Don't Yell Challah

- ❑ 1 Broomstick
- ❑ Potatoes (yeah)

INSTRUCTIONS:

In a clean garage, glue your two-inch pipe to your reducer to your four-inch pipe to your plug. You should now have what looks like a parking meter that, due to a communications mix-up at the parking meter company, does not actually have any numbers or a coin slot. The parking meter part is going to be your combustion chamber, and the pole part is going to be your barrel. The plug part is going to be your last line of defense against the gun backfiring and accidentally launching a high-velocity potato straight into your gut.

Next, sharpen the end of your barrel so that it will cleanly core a potato when you jam one in there with the broomstick. Drill a few holes toward the other end of the barrel and insert screws to act as stoppers, so that your potato doesn't fall into the combustion chamber. Drill two holes across from each other in your combustion chamber and install the barbecue lighter. You're now ready to use your potato gun. (Not right now. Take it *outside* first, for heaven's sake.)

To use the gun, simply ram in a potato or one of your denser *matzah* balls, unscrew the plug at the bottom of the combustion chamber, squirt in a short burst of hair spray or deodorant or anything with a skull and crossbones on the warning label, screw your plug back on, and ignite.

We forgot to tell you to aim it. Our apologies.

Potato guns make a fun Chol Hamoed alternative to paint ball, although your neighbor is bound to be extremely disturbed by the amount of potatoes he finds growing in his yard next year. Keep out of reach of children, and keep your potatoes locked up separately when not in use, preferably in a safe deposit box in Switzerland.

❧

Stuffed Pharaoh

Source: Cooking for Mummies

YOU WILL NEED:

- ❑ 1 Pharaoh (deceased)
- ❑ 2 buckets Nile water
- ❑ 1 wheelbarrow Manischewitz Pharaoh Stuffing
- ❑ 1 tub oil (any)
- ❑ 3 miles gauze or two-ply toilet paper
- ❑ Salt, to taste

INSTRUCTIONS:

In a clean tomb, wash your Pharaoh thoroughly. Gut Pharaoh, cover in salt, and allow to sit for forty days, with the windows open if possible. Go check on your chicken soup and sample your *cholent*.

Upon returning, insert a meat thermometer into your Pharaoh, either orally or not orally, to make sure that his body has cooled to room temperature. Wash Pharaoh again, and add sweet-smelling oils to get rid of the stench. If sweet-smelling oils are unavailable, you can substitute crude oil. Re-stuff Pharaoh, and wrap him in gauze or toilet paper until you're sufficiently certain that he can't escape. Bind his arms and legs together just in case.

Get some friends to help you move the Pharaoh into a sarcophagus, or just stamp the gauze with sufficient postage and

Don't Yell Challah

mail him to someone who owes you money. Wash your hands extremely well. Serves entire kingdom.

Chapter Seven
The Day Before Tomorrow

~ The Shabbos Before ~

Shabbos Hagadol

The Shabbos before Pesach is special. So special, in fact, that it is actually called "The Great Shabbos." That's how special it is. It is not merely the last Shabbos that you get to eat *challah* for at least two weeks. It is the Shabbos on which we observe the following great traditions:

1. On the morning of that Shabbos, we read a *haftorah* that mentions the word "Hagadol."

2. On Shabbos afternoon, we fly through the Haggadah under our breath in record time, including the part that talks about how we only read the Haggadah on Pesach itself.

3. We go to *shul* on Shabbos afternoon for the express purpose of fighting our instinct to nap while listening to the Rabbi go

into depth about a pertinent topic that often has absolutely nothing to do with Pesach. But we can't really blame him for that, because the truth is that if we would come in for a speech like this more than once a year, he would have a chance to get all these pertinent topics off his chest some other time, and then spend Shabbos Hagadol talking about something with some actual relevance to Pesach, such as how to boil our dentures.

4. We have entire Shabbos meals consisting of food that can be prepared using only a crock-pot, a travel burner, and a dairy microwave.
5. We eat these meals in the middle of the driveway.

Why is This Shabbos Different?

Shabbos Hagadol was established to commemorate the Shabbos before the very first Pesach, when the Jews brought live Paschal lambs into their homes, and then ate their Shabbos meals out on the driveway. When the rest of Egypt found out what this meant for the Egyptian firstborn, a civil war broke out between the group of Egyptians who wanted to keep the Jews in Egypt to see what would happen, and the group of Egyptians, mainly consisting of the actual firstborn, who decided that maybe it was time to let them leave. Brother fought against brother, sons fought against their fathers, and by the end of the Civil War the slaves were basically free. That is the greatness of this Shabbos.

What is interesting to note about Shabbos Hagadol is that, although all of this happened on the tenth of Nissan, we instead choose to focus on the fact that it was the second Shabbos of the month. It's one of the only days on the Jewish calendar that we commemorate on a specific day of the week, rather than on

The Day Before Tomorrow

the actual date that it occurred. The secular calendar does this all the time: Thanksgiving is always on a Thursday, Presidents' Day is always on a Monday, etc., and nobody actually cares on what date these events originally took place, so long as we get our long holiday weekend. But it turns out that is just the point of Shabbos Hagadol; we specifically keep it on the weekend, so that no one could come up with work-related excuses as to how they would really love to come to the speech but they don't have enough vacation days because they're going to be spending all eight days of Pesach at the in-laws.

THE NIGHT BEFORE

Bedikas Chometz – The Search for *Chometz*

The night before Pesach is crunch time. It is the time when someone, typically the head of the household, allows her husband to perform an inspection of the entire premises in the dark, juggling three small items, one of which is a lit candle, and trying not to set the suit closet on fire. The fact that there are three items to carry was the Rabbis' way of encouraging family participation.

Traditionally, the three items we use are a candle, a feather, and a spoon, which you can obtain at your local Judaica store, unless you want to try to track down the three items on your own, as practice. (I have no idea where you can buy a feather. I would suggest just break open a pillow, and then you'd be set for life.) The basic idea of the *bedikah* is to locate the *chometz* with your candle, which can illuminate areas of your home that the overhead lights cannot reach without a serious moving of the furniture, and then to hold the other end of the candle in your mouth while you use the feather to sweep the *chometz* onto the spoon. Then you

Don't Yell Challah

take the candle out of your mouth and put the feather in, because now you have to balance a lit candle *and* a spoon with *chometz* on it. And then you have to figure out how to fit a second piece of *chometz* onto that little wooden spoon with your feather.

So the truth is that not *everyone* actually uses the spoon, but just sort of carries it around anyway, for *kabbalistic* reasons, and instead brushes the *chometz* into a paper bag or a manila envelope or a snow shovel. I personally use a dustpan, because that way I can melt the bottom of the candle onto the pan, and I only need to hold two items, which is just as well, because I only *have* two hands, and my kids are currently too young to follow me around the house at eight o'clock at night with a spoon. But I do have to be careful about using the tiny Chanukah candles that they put in the *bedikah* kits, because if I actually want to search my house with one of those, I have to do it really quickly, or the candle will melt down and set my bread on fire. A good, thick Shabbos candle works just fine, or else I use those really tall Chanukah candles that they make for Friday nights.

What We're Looking For

Typically, we're looking for our ten pieces of bread. I am referring here to the ten pieces that the head of the household hides around the house for one purpose: So that we will find *something*. Because if she honestly thought that there was anywhere in the house that she'd forgotten to clean, then definitely she would just go clean it. You rarely hear a woman say, "Hey, you're right! I *did* forget to scrub the bottom of the fridge! Here, let me hold your candle for you while you get that. I think you're going to need a bigger feather." In fact, most wives clean so well that they insist on hiding their ten pieces of bread on little

The Day Before Tomorrow

napkins, or wrapping them in plastic, because they don't want the *bedikah* to generate crumbs, and they definitely don't think we're going to do a very good job sweeping them up with the feather. Nevertheless, the main point of the *bedikah* is not just a "Ceremony for the Rounding Up of the Bread." It is to make sure that they actually *didn't* forget to clean anything important.

But mainly we just look for the bread. There are several reasons for this, of course:

1. We don't actually *know* that there's other *chometz* around, but we do know that there's bread.

2. Assuming that we've done a somewhat decent job cleaning, chances are that anything we find will not be nearly as bad as the actual bread.

3. We are making up for our single days, when we did not actually clean our apartments or dorm rooms at all until the day before Pesach, and then did a quick cleaning-slash-*bedikah* using a flashlight, a vacuum cleaner, and a wooden spoon. But we *always* found more than ten pieces.

If, for whatever reason, you do not have anyone to hide the bread for you, you can always hide it yourself by blindly throwing a handful into your living area, and then trying to find where it all landed, or by hiding it methodically and then drinking your leftover Purim wine until you simply don't remember.

And in case you are not the type who likes to put together his own *bedikas chometz* kit, you can also buy a *bedikas chometz* kit that includes ten tiny wrapped pieces of bread for only four or five dollars more. You do *not* want to know how old that bread is.

Don't Yell Challah

Actually Finding It

Many wives wonder why, even though they hide their ten pieces of bread pretty much in plain sight, their husbands still give up after they find about seven, tops. "Are you sure you hid ten?" the husbands want to know. We could have been hot-and-cold champions in grade school, but when it comes to finding *chometz*, we're completely clueless. But that is only because of all of the stuff we're trying to juggle that effectively limits search capabilities primarily to areas that are between three and six feet off the ground.

Then there was the year that my wife decided it would be a really good idea to hide little slivers of pita bread, because pita doesn't leave any crumbs (that we can see). After searching the entire house for over an hour, I came up with maybe four pieces, because, as it turns out, pita slivers look a lot like little pieces of paper, especially by candlelight. I assume that this was a big problem for writers in the Middle Ages. So eventually, I set my candle down and picked up a flashlight, and in five minutes I had found the rest of the pita, as well as the previous year's spoon.

My point is that it is very important for us men to keep looking until we find all of it ourselves, because otherwise our wives are going to start catching on and demanding presents in exchange for telling us where all of the bread is hidden. So we've really got to put our thinking caps on, because we're talking about ten presents. Though I suspect that there is actually some secret tradition passed on from mother to daughter wherein they hide only nine pieces so that we spend all night checking every corner of the house, and when they are satisfied that we have done a thorough job, they magically produce a tenth piece from a place that we have already checked at least five times, and by then it is already…

The Day Before Tomorrow

~ The Morning Before ~

A Quick Fast

The morning before Pesach is also called *Taanis Bechorim* — the Fast of the Firstborns. It commemorates the fact that all of the Jewish firstborns were spared during the Plague of the Firstborn, as well as the fact that the Jewish firstborns of the time fasted the day before just in case. Fasting in Jewish tradition has always been a way of repenting for all of the bad things we may have done, so that instead of constantly thinking about food all the time, we can instead think about Hashem and our place in the world. Whereas nowadays, we live in a society that is used to eating just about every day, so we actually spend all of our fast days thinking about how hungry we are, and how we'd really like some food, and how everything we see looks like food, and wandering into convenience stores for a drink or a bag of chips before remembering *why* we're so hungry, and planning what we're going to eat the moment the fast is over. Come to think of it, this might be the connection to Pesach, on some level.

So the point of our fasts these days seems to be to torment ourselves for anything we may have done wrong, and then to sit around and watch the rest of the world eat and advertise juicy steaks on huge billboards in the middle of the highway right next to a farm full of cattle that luckily cannot read, and to *think about what we've done!* We are no longer at the same spiritual level that we used to be, so we need all of the repentance we can get. That is why we commemorate the ancient Fast of the Firstborns with a fast of our own, except that in our case no one actually fasts, because of:

Don't Yell Challah

The *Siyum*

It turns out that if someone participates in a *"seudas mitzvah,"* or a festive meal in honor of the completion of a significant ritual, he is allowed to break his fast in honor of that ritual, and then he can drag out his celebration and continue to eat the entire day. A *seudas mitzvah* sometimes comes in the form of a *bris*, wherein everyone gets to participate in the *seudah* except for the guest of honor, who gets to suck a drop of wine off the end of a tissue. But since it is not easy to schedule a *bris* to come out exactly when you want it to, most *shuls* generally hold a *siyum* celebrating the completion of a particular portion of the *Talmud* by someone who finished a particular tractate for like the eighth time in his life over the course of maybe the last three days. He reads off the end of the portion after the morning services, and everyone celebrates via Pesach pastries and juice in the *shul* vestibule far into the morning, although not *too* far into the morning, because there's still a lot of running around to do.

"Hey, Wait A Minute!"

"Wait a minute!" you are no doubt saying. "Since when can we just negate a fast like that? Can I cut *Yom Kippur* short too because I finished all of *Tehillim* while the *chazzan* spent the better part of the morning on a single page?"

If that is the case, I advise you to stop yelling at this book for a second and realize that *Taanis Bechorim* is not a biblical obligation. That said, there are various practical reasons as to why one should not fast on the day before Pesach, among them the fact that there is a lot to do that day, as we've mentioned, and the fact that our stomachs tend to contract when we fast, which is why we spend most fast days buying out the entire supermarket and then come

The Day Before Tomorrow

home at night and eat about half a bagel. There would be no way we could get through all of the different opinions about how much wine to drink and how much *matzah* and *marror* to eat on Pesach night and still have room for the *afikoman*. So most of us do not fast, and the entire repentance of the day comes from the fact that we are actually getting up for *shacharis* and not skipping out of it early to go start fires or search for that nonexistent tenth piece of bread.

The Midmorning Before

(DISCLAIMER: The following section discusses setting fires, and contains many explicit fire-related terms, which can be hazardous to your health. Please note that fires are dangerous, and should not be set by anyone except maybe a trained professional under controlled conditions, and even then only in dire circumstances. You don't have to care, but we are required to put this in for legal reasons.)

Burning Your *Chometz* – *Biur Chometz*

So it's the morning before Pesach, and as much as you tried to get rid of all of your *chometz* through several weird combination meals ("More bread burgers, anyone?") you are still left with a huge pile of food that has to be finished off by about ten A.M. Your only option is to somehow dispose of it all, and they've already kicked you out of the zoo for feeding the animals ketchup. Plus you have your little manila envelope containing ten small pieces of bread and a fairly nasty feather. So what most people do is they set their *chometz* on fire; and on purpose this time.

Don't Yell Challah

Setting *chometz* on fire is a tradition we have had for thousands of years, marred only occasionally by the burning down of a small European village. It is therefore very important to observe the following important fire safety guidelines:

IMPORTANT FIRE SAFETY GUIDELINES
(Brought to you by the American Dental Association)

1. Set the fire in a sturdy metal receptacle such as a dumpster or a foil pan or a trash can without a plastic liner.
2. Keep fire away from children and small animals, as well as chain smokers.
3. While tending to the fire, do not wear any flammable clothing.
4. Always stand upwind of the fire to avoid smoke inhalation. In case of a tornado, constantly circle the fire to remain upwind.
5. If you drop your marshmallow, let it go.
6. Don't try to stomp out the fire when you're done unless you have good insurance.
7. Some of the people around you are going to go find a stick and poke the fire for no particular reason. You must resist the temptation to push them in.
8. Make sure to brush your teeth before Pesach.

Once you have a fire going anyway, you can also feel free to add anything that was used on a holiday that you are not entirely sure how to dispose of, such as your *lulav*, your soggy *Chanukah* wicks (or bulbs, if you use bulbs), and your honey cake. You can also take the opportunity to cut your kids' hair and shoot at your friends with arrows that have little plungers on the ends. Or maybe we are thinking of the wrong bonfire. But you can definitely use the fire to get rid of all of the dry leaves lying around your yard

The Day Before Tomorrow

that the trash collector has refused to take in because he's not the one getting a ticket. Let's see how he feels about taking a whole can full of ashes.

It is at this point that we generally read a little Aramaic passage, in which we acknowledge that we may not have cleaned under some of the furniture, and that anything we might have missed should be considered null and/or void like the dust of the Earth, which is of culinary interest only to crawling infants, who also like eating the crumbs under your furniture, hence the comparison.

Before you start your fire, you should probably have some basic idea of what you're going to do with the remains when you're done. You may want to locate some kind of dumpster somewhere, although if you want to make a couple of bucks you can put it into a tasteful urn and sell it to the local funeral home so they can use it if they ever misplace anybody. ("All right, here is your uncle Louie. If you look inside you can still see the charred remains of the honey cake he was eating when he died.") I bring this up because my parents have a neighbor who tried to kick it into the sewer one year, but apparently he didn't really check to make sure that the fire was out, and it turns out that another neighbor had tried to bury all of his dry leaves in that same sewer to avoid a ticket. From what I heard, there were flames shooting ten feet above the grate.

Another option for *chometz* burning is to drive over to the neighborhood fire, where everyone throws their *chometz* into a huge flaming dumpster and then loses track of whether or not their particular *chometz* was consumed by the fire, and then just kind of wanders off. Nevertheless the neighborhood fires are probably not a good idea for you personally, because you have proven that you are not to be trusted with an open flame when you melted down your dustpan during the *bedikah*. These community fires were

Don't Yell Challah

requested by the firefighters, who were exhausted from all of the calls by alarmed non-Jewish neighbors looking out their windows, to which they'd respond, and then find themselves subjected to confusing conversations wherein the suspected arsonists helpfully tried to explain the concepts of "*chometz*" and "*biur*" and "*yaharog v'al ya'avor*." So now these firefighters spend a much less stressful day of keeping an *eye* on the dumpster and poking at it with approved sticks and keeping people a at safe distance and answering questions about their fire trucks and repeatedly reminding the same five people NOT TO THROW ANY PLASTIC INTO THE FIRE. But then these people wait until the fire fighters are distracted, answering questions about what kind of gas mileage their trucks get, and then they throw in their plastic bags. That'll show those anti-Semites.

Also The Midmorning Before

Magic Beans

Way back when, people usually finished off all of their *chometz* before Pesach. Nobody really had a whole lot of possessions in the first place, and there were no refrigerators, so *chometz* disposal took maybe five minutes. The biggest concern back then, and this is discussed heavily in the Talmud, was how to *kosher* all of the really old pots that were held together by large patches of stale dough.

But then the Jews started coming into possession of vast amounts of *chometz*, in the form of bakeries and kosher supermarkets and stocks in major corporations (you cannot just burn down a major corporation on *Erev* Pesach, unless that was in your initial agreement), and large amounts of liquor that were brought out mainly for *seudos mitzvah*, and which rarely got

The Day Before Tomorrow

touched because the guests who could tell the difference knew that this wasn't the type of liquor that got better with age, at least not in an opened bottle. So many people found themselves stumbling around their *bedikas chometz* drunk, because they were trying to finish as much liquor as they could before Pesach. And the *chometz* fires were *huge*.

And so the rabbis, who as a group tended to have more *seudos mitzvah* than anyone else, decided to institute the concept of "*mechiras chometz*," in which they would sell *chometz* "futures" to a non-Jew for a ridiculously low down payment, and the buyer would agree to "pay" for the rest "later," and then they'd give him a receipt for tax purposes.

The *Mechirah* Process

Basically, we sell the *chometz* to our Rabbi, who makes us fill out a form listing all of the places where we may still have *chometz*. For instance, we could write:

- Any cabinet in our house with masking tape over the door and the word "*chometz*" spelled wrong in magic marker.
- The charred *chometz* beneath the sewer grate in front of our house.
- The Nabisco cookie plant, where we own about twelve shares, and whose managers have threatened to call the cops if we keep pestering them to shut down production for a week.
- The home of Yoichie and Chani Shmeltzer, who borrowed our hand mixer over six months ago and have yet to return it. What are they mixing already? Maybe now that it's yours, they'll return it if you ask nicely.

Don't Yell Challah

After filling out the form, we hand it over to the Rabbi, who compensates us for our merchandise by handing us a belt. Or a tie. And it's not even a particularly nice tie, because he is afraid that someone will accidentally walk off with it. And we already have more ties at home than we're ever actually going to use, so what are we going to do with it? Hang ourselves? So we give it back, and then we casually slip the Rabbi some cash when we shake his hand, like he's getting us a good table at a fancy restaurant.

After the Rabbi is satisfied that he owns the *chometz* of everyone in the *shul*, he runs away to Mexico and changes his name. I'm just kidding, of course. He's a Rabbi, he doesn't do things like that. That's why we sell it to him in the first place, as opposed to selling it to, say, the treasurer. What the Rabbi actually does is he turns around and sells it to a gentile, all the while hinting, but not actually saying, that the buyer has the right to sell it all back after Pesach for a small profit after he does the legwork and realizes that dragging a U-Haul around town to pick up a bunch of rapidly aging boxes of crackers may not be fiscally worth it. Hanging out with Jews will do that to a *goy*.

RABBI: "So here is a big pile of forms (*wink, wink*), and I trust that you will pay cash for the rest of the merchandise in about a week or so (*wink, wink, nudge, nudge*)."

PROSPECTIVE BUYER: "If you don't stop elbowing me, I'm not going to buy your old food."

How It Works

No, we're not trying to pull anything past anybody. It's not like we're sitting around laughing and elbowing each other while nervously eyeing the skies and hoping not to get struck by

The Day Before Tomorrow

lightning. (We always assume Hashem is going to use lightning, because that's probably what *we* would do, as it seems to have a great comedic effect.)

The truth is that selling *chometz* is a business transaction, and not a prayer. So whether or not we mean it deep down inside, once we agree to sell something for a certain price and we sign a contract to that effect, it is considered a sale to the fullest extent. It's like when your father-in-law sells you his rapidly aging car for a dollar, purely for tax reasons. That does not make it any less yours, and if he insists on taking it back, you can calmly and nonchalantly ask him if he enjoys spending Pesach with his grandchildren.

In our case, the buyer is considered to have paid for the sale in full, and he owes the sale itself nothing — he just owes the sellers the money they laid out for him. So even if he knows that he will sell it back later, the truth is that if he suddenly did get struck by lightning over Pesach, it will be up to his kids to decide whether to keep all of the *chometz*, and if there was no life insurance they may just choose to go with the U-Haul idea.

That Said

That said, your Rabbi is going to want to sell the *chometz* to a *goy* with a *mesorah* — that is, a tradition passed down from father to son about how the sale is done, and whether it is a good idea to start eating all the *chometz* that very afternoon if he wants the Rabbi to continue using him in the future. But once in a while, the Rabbi is going to come across someone he has not dealt with before, and will have to contend with a major barrage of questions:

"What? Aren't you supposed to be like a Rabbi or something?"

Don't Yell Challah

"So you're saying this food isn't kosher?"

"What's the catch? Because I don't want to do this with you if you're going to change your mind in a week."

"I don't understand one word you just said. Can I keep it, or what?"

"I thought Jews were supposed to be *smart* businessmen."

"I think I should call my attorney. Should I call my attorney? He's Jewish."

On the other hand, sometimes it can be harder to work with your more experienced buyers:

EXPERIENCED BUYER: "Look, you've got some *chometz* you want to get rid of. Now I don't really want your *chometz*. I've got plenty of *chometz* at home, and I have some inside information that Shop-Rite is going to have a major sale over Pesach. But I can see that you're a nice Rabbi, and I'm willing to buy the whole lot for, let's see…(*he flips through the stack of forms*) five dollars."

RABBI: "Five dollars? We can *burn* it for less than five dollars!"

EXPERIENCED BUYER: "Then you can take your business elsewhere. Good luck explaining the process."

RABBI: "All right, listen. We don't really want to sell it to you. There are a lot of *goyim* around with a *mesorah*. And that homeless person over there just said that he would give us ten dollars worth of bottles and cans, plus he'd clean our cars for Pesach. But you look like a nice *goy*… I mean guy. So what do you say?"

This goes back and forth for a while, until eventually both parties come to some sort of agreement, at which point they draw up a deed of sale.

The Day Before Tomorrow

Memorandum Of Conformity Of Agreement Of Sale

Made and entered into by and between

Rabbi I.M. Exhausted

(Hereinafter referred to as the Seller)

and

Bob Shaigetz

(Hereinafter referred to as the Purchaser, unless we forget)

E. Pluribus Unum

This document certifies that the Seller has agreed, on behalf of all of his congregants, especially those who will be away for the holidays and pretty much did not bother cleaning *at all*, to sell all of the *chometz* listed within enclosed forms therein for the Holy down payment of:

Seven dollars and fifty cents

Which, he assures the Purchaser, is a great deal.

In addition, the Purchaser agrees to:

Turn the lights on in the shul on two Shabbosim to be named later.

The congregants will also have the legal right to open up their closets in cases of extreme necessity, such as that they accidentally locked one or more of their kids in there. **Bob** hereby certifies that he is a *goy*, and that he will not come in and make himself a sandwich during *Ha lachma anya*.

Carpe Diem   Cogito Ergo Sum

Shivisi Hashem Linegdi Samid

Ne'um: **Yankel Schwartz,** Eid   Ne'um: **John Hancock,** Eid

Don't Yell Challah

~~THE DAY BEFORE IF IT IS A SHABBOS~~

The *Really* Big Shabbos

When the day before Pesach is on a Shabbos, at least four issues arise:

- You cannot perform the *bedikah* on Friday night, because you can't carry around a candle, and it is very impractical to just look for *chometz* in the kitchen and the living area and around the little nightlight in the bathroom.

- You cannot actually burn your *chometz* on Shabbos morning, unless that was one of the conditions you made with your *goy*.

- Everyone goes into a panic about how they can possibly have *seudah shlishis*, or the third Shabbos meal, which we generally eat on Shabbos afternoon, and which most people usually have in *shul* because otherwise they would probably just skip it altogether. But people who don't think about *seudah shlishis* all year suddenly go crazy about it the day before Pesach. The problem, as it turns out, is that: A) we're not supposed to eat a large meal, defined as any meal involving some kind of bread and some kind of fish with some kind of horseradish-slash-mayonnaise dressing too close to the Passover Seder, B) We could try to have it in the morning, but that is technically when we are eating our *second* Shabbos meal, which includes all of the above plus *cholent*, which we absolutely cannot miss because it's bad enough we can't put any beans into it as we are all cleaned for Pesach already, C) Even if we could cram in another meal after the *cholent*, assuming you can cram *anything* in after *cholent*, the third meal is technically supposed to be

The Day Before Tomorrow

eaten in the afternoon, D) Cramming it in is not going to be easy, because we're supposed to finish all of our bread by about Ten A.M., and E) *Matzah* on Erev Pesach is out of the question, because you won't be excited about the *matzah* at the Seder, although considering how long it's been since you've eaten anything by the time the *matzah* comes, you would probably be excited to eat your own pillow at the Seder.

- Every time this happens there is a sudden influx of books that climb over each other to explain what you should do, and none of them agree, because when it comes to Shabbos Erev Pesach no one can quite remember what his grandfather used to do, so you are stuck trying to decide which book to get, and cannot for the life of you recall whether you bought one the last time this happened. That said, I would like to take this opportunity to thank you from the bottom of my heart for choosing *this* book, because, in all fairness, it's going to prove to be the least helpful of the lot.

- You are not supposed to fast on Shabbos. (This is not as much of an issue because: A) Most people aren't firstborns, and B) Most firstborns don't fast anyway. They just have a *siyum*, which, if done correctly, may count as one of their Shabbos meals.)

These are indeed some major issues. As such, I have spent a lot of time reading all of the other books in order to provide you with a basic idea of what most people seem to do. (This is bearing in mind that if you copy from one person it is plagiarism, but if you copy from many people, it's research.)

Don't Yell Challah

First of all, *Ta'anis Bechorim* is pulled back to Thursday, because we're not supposed to fast on Friday either, so that we won't go into Shabbos hungry. This is despite the fact that, as we mentioned, no one actually fasts on *Ta'anis Bechorim* anyway.

The search for the *chometz* is pulled back to Thursday night, so that we can burn everything on Friday morning (even though we can technically eat *chometz* afterward), so that we don't get confused the next year about how come we didn't have a bonfire last year, and what did our grandfather do?

In regards to the Shabbos meals, what a lot of people do is they pray early on Shabbos morning, so that they can begin their second meal early, eat a bit of bread and maybe some fish, take a break, and then start another bread meal, all so that they will be eating their *cholent* no later than ten A.M. They also have a light snack later on in the day, so that they can say that they ate something in the afternoon.

And as for the bread/*matzah* problem, some people go with Passover egg *matzah*, which they cannot use for the Seder anyway, because there is a slight chance that egg *matzah* can *never* become *chometz* (unless you make it *gebroktz*, of course). Others save a little bit of non-crummy *chometz* bread, such as pita or bagels, and eat it out on the porch, and then perform *biur chometz* by flushing the leftovers down the toilet, praying that their plastic bags do not suddenly decide to back it up. Those anti-Semites.

Chapter Eight
Seder Up

The Seder Table

Having a well-set table is essential for your enjoyment of the Pesach Seder. Setting your table properly can mean the difference between a deeply spiritual experience wherein all of the generations of the family enjoy each others' company and share meaningful insights into the fundamental questions of life and Judaism and grow together physically, spiritually, and emotionally, and a Seder table at which everyone is leaning into *every* else's lap and all of the lefties are sitting between all of the righties and there are three or four Seder plates fighting for space at one end of the table and *every* time someone turns a page the *matzos* crack a little.

So one of your big concerns is space. The Pesach Seder can take up a lot of space, especially if your family has a tendency to line dance around the table during *Echad Mi Yodeia*. If your home is not big enough, and you find yourself having to figure

Don't Yell Challah

out interesting ways to snake folding tables around corners, down hallways, up flights of stairs, etc., you may just want to hold the entire Seder out on your front lawn, although that would make opening the door for Eliyahu interesting, as if you're letting him *out* of the house. Also, there is no way you would ever find the *afikoman*. ("What do you mean, 'I think someone walked off with it?'")

Once you have your tables properly positioned and you've put out enough chairs, folding chairs, beach chairs, step stools, stacks of phone books, etc., your next step is to arrange the following items on it in a practical yet space-efficient manner:

- Cups – To be used throughout the Seder. These cups can be silver, or that plated silver that they sell at closeout stores that dissolves in contact with silver polish. You can even use glasses, or mugs with "World's Best *Bubby*" emblazoned on the side. Many *Haggados* show a picture of four cups lined up in a row on the cover. I don't know about you, but I usually just use the same cup four times. It just makes things easier all around, especially in terms of space, and the ramifications of shaking the table. But it may be a good idea to have them lined up like that if your plan is to finish the Seder in record time.

- Saucers – Saucers are usually a good idea too, because there is one part of the Seder when everyone pours a little bit of wine out of their cups, and without saucers it can get messy, especially if you are concerned about *gebruktz*. And never mind what it could do to your *kittel*.

- Adequate Supply of napkins – Of course.

Seder Up

- *Kittel* – A lot of married men have the custom to wear a *kittel*, which looks sort of like a coat worn by a nursing home *mashgiach* or the guy trapped in the meat freezer in the back of the supermarket, although *kittels* tend to be more frilly. On the first night of Pesach, the *kittel* is white, and on the second night it is the same color as whichever wine you've been drinking, because not everyone has the leaning thing down. The whiteness of the *kittel* symbolizes purity, (except for the second night, when it symbolizes wine), and is also worn to the synagogue on Yom Kippur, although if you don't get it dry cleaned by then, a lot of people may assume that it's blood, and you might be asked to leave. (And if you actually get your *kittel* dirty on Yom Kippur itself, you're probably using it wrong.) *Kittels* are also worn under the wedding canopy, and most people are buried in them as well. (And no, I am not going to make the obvious joke. You're just going to have to make it yourself.)

  SIDE NOTE: When I got married, my grandmother showed up at the wedding with a bottle of the whitest wine she could find, so that we wouldn't ruin my seventy-five dollar *kittel* and my wife's thousand-dollar wedding dress. (And at this point I would like to point out that I have worn my *kittel* at least twice a year since then, not counting the Purim that I dressed up as a doctor, and my wife has not worn her wedding dress at all, not even to other people's weddings.)

- *Pillows* – Depending on who's running the Seder, you're going to want to set up some pillows.

  Okay, that came out wrong. What we meant was, the person running the Seder is going to need some pillows to lean on, and depending on the customs of everyone involved, some of the other guests may need them too. A

Don't Yell Challah

few weeks before school your child's teacher may request that you send in a clean white pillowcase for your child to decorate, although why the teacher seems to think that you have any clean white pillowcases is beyond us. Most of the spare pillowcases in your house are either festooned with pictures of Big Bird, or have huge unexplained beige spots on them. And if you did manage to come across a clean white pillowcase, the last thing you'd want is for your kids to color all over it. Maybe you can just put last year's pillowcase through the laundry and send it in again. Or you can just flip it like a couch cushion and decorate the other side.

- *Afikoman* **Bags** – Every family at your Seder table will require an *afikoman* bag, because hiding the *afikoman* is a fun activity that will keep the children awake in anticipation of the moment that their father decides that he's too tired to bother looking for it, and instead elects to show his children the side of him that negotiated for their tuition. And some children fall asleep after they hide it anyway, so you have to just get another *matzah* from the box and find the *afikoman* in the morning. Many children will make an *afikoman* bag in school too, but because of school budget cuts you will not be able to fit the bigger half of your *matzah* into the bag, and will have to break it into tiny shards, many of which will fall out and leave a trail of tiny crumbs to wherever your children hid the *afikoman*.

- *Haggados* – Everyone is probably going to need his or her own Haggadah, and they will be very specific about which one they want, so you should not even bother putting them out. Some guests will want Haggadahs that feature lots of commentaries that they can share, or else read to pass the time while the kids repeat the same *divrei* Torah that they

Seder Up

said last year and last night and that all of the other children at the table said not three minutes ago. Other guests will want *Haggados* that won't require them to keep turning pages, because who knows what turning fourteen pages per minute will do to the *matzos*. If it were up to them, the entire Haggadah would be formatted to fit onto one big laminated page, like a *bentcher*.

- Once upon a time, there were only five types of *Haggados* around. There was the one that looked like a *Mikraos Gedolos Chumash*; the one that had lots of paintings of anatomically impossible Israelites holding Sedarim where everyone seems to be sitting in a dense clot with no room for their legs, and Pharaoh making a face like he's eating *marror*; there was also the Haggadah that was sponsored by Maxwell House ("The Official Haggadah of Keeping You Awake at the Seder"); there was the original Artscroll Haggadah, which translated everything in a way that was *not* vaguely heretical; and there was the one with the Yiddish *Ma Nishtana*. But then at some point the market got flooded with Haggados for people of every age, background, and religion. We have The Youth Haggadah, The Old People Haggadah (featuring about six enormous words per page), The Family Haggadah, The Single Guy Haggadah, the Haggadah of the Roshei Yeshiva, The Haggadah of the Guy Who Sits in the Back of the Beis Midrash Who Never Learns What Everyone Else is Learning, The Questions Asked Haggadah, The Ask Questions Haggadah (for the *She'eino Yodea Lishol*), The Haggadah 'From Dusk until Dawn,' The Haggadah 'From Nine-Thirty Until About a Quarter to Two,' The 'We Almost Could Have Won' Haggadah for Egyptians, The 'We Missed the Whole Thing' Haggadah for Hare Krishnas, The Haggadah Du Francais Du Scrolle Du Art, and

Don't Yell Challah

the Polish Haggadah Shel Sukkos. In fact, if you so choose, you can go through your entire life never having to use the same Haggadah twice, although you are going to have to significantly expand your Pesach cabinet.

Preparing the Symbolic Foods

Once you have everything set up and you weigh down the laminated *Haggados* so they don't blow away, it's time to start on the symbolic Seder foods. On Pesach Night, we are obligated to feel as if we are actually going out of Mitzrayim, and since four hundred years of slavery and ten national disasters would require sizeable budget and a whole lot more preparation time than just the thirty days since Purim, we instead just eat a lot of foods to help us *pretend* that we are living through it. "Wow, that is some powerful *marror*! Now I know exactly how our ancestors felt!" So we see right off the bat that there is more going on than we understand. Also, the original Exodus didn't come with a wine list.

Choosing a Wine

In preparation for the Seder, you're going to want to pick a really good wine that compliments your Poor Man's Bread. Most commentators suggest that you drink *red* wine, which symbolizes freedom, as opposed to white wine, which symbolizes fish. Also, red wine goes best with *kittels*.

But that doesn't narrow it down much. If you open up the average wine list you will see that that there are actually *hundreds* of types of red wine, all with increasingly foreign names, which, when translated, often means something mundane, like, "wine of the bottle." Sometimes you can tell what it is by the description, but often it seems that the actual descriptions have nothing to

Seder Up

do with the wine, and were written by professional wine tasters after an entire day of tasting wine after wine after wine, and then staggering home and sitting down in front of the microwave to try to type something along the lines of, *"This wine is from the Eastern Regions of New Jersey, cut about two-thirds of the way into the first harvest, and has a distinct grapey smell. One can also detect essences of apples, rubbing alcohol, cotton candy, and grass. The wine also has a vague spicy-peach flavor, which is weird, because they don't let peaches anywhere near the factory."*

A lot of people, seeing as they're going to be drinking an upwards of four cups in one sitting during which their most strenuous activity will be trying to hit the high notes in *Vehi She'amdah*, generally try to go with somewhat of a light wine that has slightly less kick than apple juice. Other people mix their wine with grape juice, in order to achieve a taste that is not quite the taste of "freedom," but more like the taste of "ruined grape juice." Rav Yonah, who lived in the times of the Talmud, drank four cups of straight wine and had a headache until Shavuos, but it turns out that Jewish wines have since improved. For instance, he did not have Rashi. Or Abarbenel. Or Akiba Eger. It always bothered me that, here we have these great men who made major contributions to Judaism, and the way that we remember their accomplishments is by naming wines after them. (Except for the Brisker Rav, who has tea, and the Bostoner, who has baked beans, and that Quaker Chassid, who has Life Cereal.) At least presidents get their pictures printed on money. Can you imagine if money had pictures of rabbis on it? All the conspiracy nuts would come out of the woodwork. So maybe sticking to wine is not so bad.

There are many other popular wines that people drink on Pesach. In fact, I could come up with a whole wine list and make fun of their names, but it would soon become obvious that I am

Don't Yell Challah

an uncultured slouch, because all of these names are new to me. I am a grape juice guy, which means that I get all excited every time they come out with a new flavor of sparkling grape juice, but it also means that my entire knowledge of wine is pretty much limited to anything called "*Kal*," as well as Cream Pink, Cream Red, Cream Malaga, the vague concept of "dry wine," and those blue bottles they put out at *sheva brachos*. In fact, I'm not even sure why they're called "dry wines." If someone knocks over a bottle, does he get you all dry? My wife, who is slightly more cultured than I am, tells me that "dry wine" is actually wine that has no sugar in it. I guess that would make it *diet* wine.

Choosing Your *Matzos*

Once you pick out your wine, you're also going to need to pick out your *matzos*. If your custom calls for square *matzos* at the Seder, this process is simple enough; square-*matzah* manufacturers are so confident in the stability of their product that they actually package them standing upright. If round *matzos* were packaged like this, the bottom end of each *matzah* would be perfectly mashed down to conform to the bottom of the box. As it is, one generally has to go through quite a few boxes to come up with three whole *matzos*. Ideally, these *matzos* would come wrapped in packing peanuts, but as we all know, peanuts are *kitniyos*. (That was a corny joke.)

But I mean it. Many packing peanuts these days actually contain cornstarch, in order to make them biodegradable, because as it is no one's entirely sure how to dispose of them. Many people leave them outside in the box they came in to be picked up by the cardboard fairy, even though they definitely are not cardboard. But now that they're cornstarch, you can scatter them all over

Seder Up

your lawn, and by next year you'll have corn, unless you mow your grass once in a while.

But that is not the point. The point is that round *matzos* are more fragile than newborn babies, and if you don't believe me, you can try holding a *matzah* by one end and smacking it on the bottom. And for the Seder, it is preferable to use the most perfect *matzos* you have, with no cracks or folds or creases. (Machine *matzos* will generally not have any creases or folds, and if they do, chances are you have a leak in your basement.)

Your Seder Plate (and you)

Next up, you're going to want to think about your Seder plate. There are a lot of symbolic foods on Pesach, and if you don't put it on some kind of Seder plate, chances are that you're going to get to the part of the Seder wherein you point at the various items, and, realizing that you've forgotten to set out the item that you're up to, you may find yourself pointing vaguely toward the kitchen.

There are many different customs as to what goes on the Seder plate, and *where*. Some plates have all of the items arranged in a circle, with the *matzos* and the salt water off to the side, but definitely not near each other. Others have the items set up in an upside down pentagon with the *marror* in the middle, and the *matzos* in a little cloth file folder. Still others have their *matzos* in a shiny metal cabinet, with the other items set up on top, out of reach of the children. Other have the Seder plate set up on little legs on top of the cloth *matzah* folder, and try not to breathe until it's time to remove the plate and eat the *matzos*. Others put the *matzos* in the middle of the plate, with the other items perched precariously around them. Others place all of the items directly on the top *matzah*, except for the salt water, because it keeps getting

Don't Yell Challah

absorbed. Others put some items on top of the *matzah*, some items under the *matzah*, and some items on the Seder plate of the person to their immediate right. And some people just buy a Seder plate and go, "Hey! I guess *this* is our *minhag* now!"

But whichever way is currently your custom, the point is to have everything clearly labeled, as opposed to forgoing the Seder plate altogether and putting everything into one big bowl and, over the course of the Seder, basically pointing out objects in a salad. ("These crunchy things are *matzah* that we eat…Why? Because we were rushed out of Mitzrayim, etc.")

Z'ROA (SHANKBONE) (look it up)

The *z'roa*, which represents the Paschal sacrifice, dates back to some time after the destruction of the Temple. Before that, they used actual sheep. (Seder plates were a lot bigger in those days.) They roasted the sheep on spits in old-fashioned ovens, which were made out of clay, and did not have Sabbath Mode. Nowadays, instead of an actual sheep, we generally use some kind of arm or wing, which has the added plus of symbolizing the mighty, outstretched arm of Hashem that took us out of Mitzrayim. Others use a chicken neck; I would guess, to symbolize that Hashem stuck out His neck for us. Granted, a wing is not an outstretched arm, but a neck is not an arm at all. But on the other hand, just as humans use our arms to pick things up, chickens actually use their necks. And besides, a chicken neck looks more like a human arm than a wing does. Not that we have any idea what Hashem's arm would look like, but we like to think it wouldn't look like a chicken wing.

Once we have our wing (or neck or shank bone) the proper thing to do is to roast it on the stove or *kashered* barbecue until it's golden brown, or darkish brown, or brownish black. It really doesn't matter, because we're not supposed to eat it.

BEITZAH (EGG)

The egg is placed on the Seder plate to commemorate the *chagigah* sacrifice, which our forefathers brought along with the Paschal lamb to try and balance out the other side of the Seder plate. The *chagigah* was eaten first, in order to assure that the Pesach sacrifice would be eaten "*al hasovah*" – when they were already full. Nowadays, many of us try to accomplish this by eating the egg. Those who do eat it usually dip it in the salt water, thus effectively changing the *Mah Nishtana*.

"Wait a minute," our children ask. "How come we're dipping a *third* time?"

"Because it tastes good," we say. Unless we forgot to boil it.

The egg also represents the Jews themselves, who get tougher under oppressive heat. After being incubated in Mitzrayim for a two hundred years, we broke out of our shells and plunged straight into the sea, where we were fought over by a bunch of hungry Egyptians with pitchforks.

MARROR (HORSERADISH) (WITHOUT BEETS)

The *marror*, which looks like a large, mutant carrot with a skin condition, is both bitter and sharp. Throughout the generations, our foremothers took the time to grate the *marror* on small metal graters, all the while sobbing, "*L'shem mitzvas marror.*" And then our forefathers and our forebrothers and sisters would walk in, take a huge whiff, shudder, and say, "This is nothing compared to last year."

The key is of course to choose the right root. I have no idea how to do this, but I have no idea how to choose a good honeydew

Don't Yell Challah

either; I thump them, knock on them, roll them down the aisle; I even shake them and put them up to my ear, as if I even know what I'm supposed to be hearing if it's ripe. A ticking sound? I don't know. But I have even more trouble picking a horseradish. The problem is that they *all* look like they've gone bad. You can try asking the produce guy at the supermarket, but chances are he doesn't know either, and he'll probably just lead you to the jarred stuff, which is produced at a horseradish-processing factory. I've always tried to picture the scene at these horseradish factories — employees writhing around on the ground, constantly running out of the building and rubbing their eyes, and the manager walking in and going, "This is nothing compared to last year. But I can't feel my face."

But the key is to pick the best fresh *marror* that you can find. Your better *marrors* will actually burn a hole right through your kitchen table and fall into the basement.

Many people nowadays, because we are weak little shells who can't handle simple things like walking ten miles barefoot in the snow to do laundry in a river that is frozen over, can never in a million years handle manually grating a vegetable that can actually tarnish silver. If you are one of these people, you have two basic options:

1. Lean back and grate it with your feet. You're going to need an amazing amount of manual dexterity, but at the end of the day the *marror* won't even taste any different.
2. Invest in a Pesach food processor, turn it on, and run out of the room. Then, using two ten-foot poles, dump the contents into a jar, seal it, and put it in the fridge.

Another problem that some people have with *marror* is the same problem they have with potato *kugel* — the minute you grate it, it starts turning brown. There are many ways to combat

Seder Up

this, but whatever you do, don't do what my mother did one year and put lemon juice in it. The way my science-oriented brother-in-law later explained it to me one Shabbos during our half-hour walk home from *shul* in the sticks, lemon juice is an acid and *marror* is a base, and if you mix an acid and a base, you get salt. So basically, my mother made salt. It was horrible, and not in the way *marror should* be horrible. If she would have added water, we could have dipped our *karpas* into it.

CHAZERES (ROMAINE LETTUCE) (WITHOUT BUGS)

This is the other category of *marror* that people generally use, although according to the Mishnah, this is actually preferable. But many people don't feel comfortable actually calling it *marror* if it can't make a grown man cry. That said, a lot of people just use it for their *Korech* sandwiches, and as their Emergency Backup *Marror*, in case for some reason their Main *Marror* tastes like salt.

The most difficult part of preparing the *chazeres* is checking the lettuce for bugs. In fact, I think that the fact that it's infested with bugs is a big part of the bitterness of romaine lettuce. In most families, the men end up doing this job, probably because if the women did it, then every time they found a bug they would call us in to stomp on it. But most of the bugs that I've found were usually dead anyway, or at least stunned by the bright light that I'm using to check for them. That said, I think that I, too, would be freaked out if I peered at a leaf with my big magnifying glass and found a family of bugs sitting around and having a Seder. (The bugs' Passover commemorates the sudden miraculous abundance of food for the locusts during the "Plague of Egyptians Wielding Rolled Up Newspapers.")

One has to be careful in searching for lettuce bugs, because some of them are very hard to see, some of them look like dirt,

Don't Yell Challah

and some of them are the same color as the lettuce. The simplest approach is to drop a handful of spiders into the bag, wait for them to eat all the bugs, and then just check for spiders, which are a lot bigger and easier to find. But what most people do is they simply look for the bugs under a bright light, and when they find one, they circle it with a red magic marker as they would Waldo.

I'm just kidding. I don't know what your particular lettuce checker does with them. You should probably ask.

CHAROSES (CHAROSES)

There's nothing like *charoses* to change *marror* from a bitter, sharp food to a bitter sharp food that looks like you dropped it in cement. To achieve this "grounded" look (sorry), you might try mixing the following ingredients, along with anything else you happen to find lying around the house:

- ❏ Ground apples
- ❏ Ground walnuts
- ❏ Ground filberts
- ❏ Ground cinnamon
- ❏ Ground wine
- ❏ Pieces of actual ground

In addition, some Sefardic Jews add figs, grapes, and pomegranates, because these are all items to which the Jews are often compared. I think that there's no reason that you cannot do the same if you want to, bearing in mind that the Jews are also compared to sand. And of course eggs.

KARPAS (AND SALT WATER)

The *karpas*, which is usually a vegetable that tastes good in salt water, is eaten to remind us of the *d'var* Torah that we've heard

Seder Up

every year since the Exodus about *"samech perach."* The salt water itself represents the sweat and tears that went into hundreds of years of Jewish labor. Many Jews of European descent use potatoes for *karpas*, once they're already using potatoes for everything else, while others may use anything from parsley to celery to raw onions, for those who want to add their own tears. Some commentaries note that, at the end of a day of hard labor, the Jews would eat a therapeutic vegetable called *"karpas,"* which was, in all likelihood, not a baked potato.

Although some versions of the Seder plate have an additional compartment for the salt water, most have discontinued this custom, because it kept leaking into the *charoses*.

MA NISHTANA CANDLES

Finally, some have a custom, on the night of the Seder, to light special *"Ma Nishtana"* candles.

Why? You may ask.

Exactly.

Chapter Nine
Funny You Should Ask

DISCLAIMER: We are about to embark on a journey through the Seder (hold on to your religious headgear), and although in general I've been bending over backwards to mention *every* Pesach custom that anyone I know has ever heard of, from this point on I will concentrate specifically on customs that I have seen with my own *eyes* at one of the Sedarim that I have actually been to, which include the Sedarim at my parents' house, my grandparents' house, my aunt and uncle's house, and my in-laws. (The one that was by far the most different was definitely my in-laws'.)

I'm mainly saying this because I don't want to receive angry letters written by people who are offended because I didn't make fun of them. "What about *my* customs?" they will ask. "You don't think they're strange? I carry a live sheep around the table on my shoulders while singing *"Chad Gadya,"* and then my kids chase me with a cat!"

Don't Yell Challah

But I don't know your custom. I've never been to your house for a Seder, and I'm never going to, because I don't *mish*. It becomes an issue when you're writing a book like this and you don't *mish*.

I only mention this because a big thing about the Seder is that, like everything else that is Pesach-related, every family has its own customs about *everything*, and everyone thinks that everyone else's customs are silly. In addition, not everyone is really sure about their own customs to begin with. They spend at least half the Seder arguing over what they did last year, and the rest arguing over whether or not what they did last year was even correct in the first place. And no one bothered to commit anything to memory last year, because we kept saying that this year we'd be in Jerusalem.

ANOTHER DISCLAIMER, WHILE WE'RE AT IT: In addition, there are parts of the Seder that we are going to touch on, and other parts that we are not going to. If this is a problem for you, you should probably also pick up a *real* Haggadah, which is not hard to come by. There are certainly enough varieties out there. And if you can't get your hands on a real Haggadah, you can even find it in most Passover prayer books, taking up something like six whole pages somewhere in the middle.

Sharing Your Food

A lot of people enjoy having guests over for the Seder, mainly to help them finish off their *charoses*, because one apple makes way more *charoses* than you're ever going to eat. In fact, some people have so many guests that they have to draw up place cards, like at a wedding, ("___Cousin Izzy___, please be seated in front of Seder Plate Number _4_") and everyone at the table

Funny You Should Ask

has to lean in unison. But if you're having company, you should make sure that you know what kind of customs your guests are used to, because they're definitely going to clash with your own. I mean it. My parents' customs have changed at least five times since I've gotten married, and I'm not sure how that happened. Even stranger, they don't even remember that they've changed anything. I only noticed because I'm not there every year, and also because lately I've been writing things down for the purposes of my book. So you should make sure to ask your guests about their customs, and to try not to laugh or ridicule them. ("You do *what?* How do you get the horseradish off the ceiling?")

Sharing Your Wisdom

But no matter how many guests you have, the focal point of the Seder has to be your children. The Seder is all about teaching your children the history of the Jewish people, and they can't very well be learning about the history of the Jewish people if they are chasing each other with pillows in the living room. Or if they're asleep, for that matter. And it doesn't help that Daylight Savings Time always comes right before Pesach, so that we all change our clocks without having the faintest idea why, and instead of starting our Seder at around eight o'clock, we start it at nine. Personally, I think we should come up with something called Pesach Seder Time (PST), which is when we temporarily pull our clocks back to regular Standard Time, so that we could start our Seder earlier. Better yet, we should pull the clocks back by about six hours so that it will be totally dark outside by three in the afternoon, and we could start our Seder then, and maybe get to sleep earlier, because we will be exhausted from getting up at two in the morning to burn our *chometz*.

Don't Yell Challah

So we definitely have to do something to keep our children awake and interested. Some parents have their kids take naps during the afternoon, and kudos to them if the kids actually sleep instead of poking their heads out of their bedrooms every time the front door opens and closes. If your kids don't sleep, there are still numerous ways of keeping them awake for the Seder, such as telling them a scary story right before bed and then waiting in the dining room with the table set until they come out to tell you that they're scared. There are also stories of rabbis in the olden days who used to study Torah through the night on a regular basis, and, in order to keep themselves awake, they would stick their feet in a bowl of cold water. In fact, in some communities, people still do this on Shavuos night. So this would definitely be a good idea for anyone who wants to keep himself awake through the end of the Seder. In fact, back when everyone was poor, this was how they used to make salt water.

In addition, the Talmud suggests giving your kids candy on Pesach Night, so that they'll ask you why. "Why Daddy why? Why? Why Mommy why? Why Mommy why Daddy why?" The idea is to get them so hopped up on sugar that they are literally bouncing off the walls, and they don't even have to hide the *afikoman*; they can just hold it and run around in circles and you *still* won't be able to catch them.

The other point of provoking their inquisitive natures, of course, is to make the Seder more interesting for them. People are generally more interested in something if they have asked a question about it than if you are just talking randomly in their direction. Take men and women for example. A woman can talk in her husband's general direction for hours; about who she saw that day, and what they said, and how they said it, and what she said back, and what she *should* have said back, and what the kids did, and what *they* said, and why none of them are wearing what they were wearing this morning, and about how the laundry basket is full again. Meanwhile, her husband, who has so far not asked a single question, and in fact had no idea that this is not what his children were wearing this morning, does not hear a word that she's saying. The entire thought process running through his head during this whole conversation goes something like this: "Supper. I'm eating supper. Supper supper supper. Ketchup? Supper supper." In the meantime, he is keeping his ears peeled for key words that involve matters that he agrees have something to do with him, such as Shabbos plans and problems with the car. And that is why a few days later he will sometimes ask a question that his wife has actually answered two days earlier while he was eating chicken cutlets. Whereas women often badger men for not telling them anything, and when they do, their men say, "Okay, so what do you want to know?" Because now we know that they're listening. And do you know *why* they're listening? Because they've asked a question.

And then of course, there is the general tendency of Jews to ask questions in the first place. Wherever there are Jews, questions abound:

"When did we eat meat?"

"What time did Shabbos start?"

"You paid *how* much?"

"But is it a *hot Kiddush*?"

"What kind of question is that?"

"*Mincha*?"

"Oh, you're from Brooklyn. Do you know the Weissmans?"

Don't Yell Challah

Therefore, a lot of the strange things we do at the Seder, we do for the sole purpose of trying to get our children to ask why. Kids love asking why. Especially little kids:

"Daddy, why do you have hair on your face?"

"Because I didn't have a chance to shave this morning."

"Why?"

"Because I was up late last night."

"Why?"

"Because I was working on my book."

"Why?"

"Because I have a deadline."

"Why?"

"Because the book has to be ready by Pesach."

"Why?"

"Because it's a book *about* Pesach."

"Why?"

"I guess I figured I should write something that people can relate to, and that didn't require a whole lot of research."

"Why?"

"So I can sell a lot of copies as quickly as possible."

"Why?"

"So I can afford to send you to school."

"Why?"

"So that ultimately you'll stop asking so many questions."

Funny You Should Ask

"Why?"

"Because you're driving me up the wall."

"Why?"

"Because as an adult, it bothers me that you won't stop asking why."

"Why?"

"I don't know. I guess at some point in life you just get used to the fact that you don't always get all the answers you want, and you stop asking so many questions."

"Why?"

"Why indeed, son. Why indeed."

So we see that a side benefit of kids asking questions is that it gets you to take a long, hard look at things. If not for my children, for example, I never would have realized that the real reason that I sometimes don't shave is that I am bothered by the fact that I have lost the innocence of youth, when I was free to ask as many questions as I could think of, and not be required by the conventions of society to either shave completely or grow a beard.

Also, in order to keep the children awake, some of their *rebbis* and *morahs* will give them as many *divrei* Torah as they can pile on. *Divrei* Torah (*dvar* Torah in singular) are interesting points that are spoken out on matters relating to the Torah (or Haggadah), that the other people would not necessarily know just by reading it themselves unless they have a Haggadah where you have to flip thirty or forty pages just to get through that part at the beginning where it lists the 15 steps of the Seder. Many teachers go through the Haggadah with their class, and generally give them short, cute *divrei* Torah, in question and answer format, as is our theme.

Don't Yell Challah

Now I want to start off by saying that I love *divrei* Torah. To me, *divrei* Torah are the heart of the Seder, often shedding a new light on points that we may have taken for granted through years of repeating the Haggadah, and that were right there in front of our faces the whole time. *Divrei* Torah can really make the Haggadah come alive. The more *divrei* Torah, the better. But you can only shed any specific light on the Haggadah so many times. If you hear the same *dvar* Torah every year for your entire childhood, and then you send your children to school and they come home with the same *dvar* Torah because their teacher has been using the same withered notebook ever since he started teaching, and that notebook has been passed down from teacher to teacher ever since your *grandparents* were in school, and at some point one of the teachers made photocopies of it (teachers are great at making photocopies) and every teacher in the Western Hemisphere is now giving out the same *divrei* Torah so that not only do all of your kids have the same *divrei* Torah, but all of your nephews and nieces do too, and they all take turns saying the same thing because none of them are paying attention when the other kids are saying it, and now you are listening to the fifth child in a row recite from his notes how "*Karpas*" stands for "*Samech Perach*" without having the foggiest idea what that has to do with anything, and yet you are expected to say, "Really? I did not know that!" in a full encouraging fashion that behooves you as a parent and will hopefully not turn the children into bitter adults like you, who don't want to hear the same seven *divrei* Torah over and over and over. Some kids will even say their entire repertoire on both nights. (And you thought it was a great idea to give them all that candy.)

If you have children in *yeshiva*, here are some of the things you are going to learn over the course of the Seder:

1. What the word "*Karpas*" stands for.

Funny You Should Ask

2. Why "*Ha Lachma Anya*" is written in Aramaic.
3. How the five rabbis didn't really have to lean, but they did anyway.
4. Why Rebbi Elazar Ben Azayah had a white beard.
5. What the "*Vehi*" in "*Vehi Sheamdah*" stands for.
6. Why we pour wine out of our cups for the *makkos*.
7. What the "*Dtzach Adash B'Achav*" stands for. (This one is pretty much spelled out in the Haggadah itself, but every kid is bowled over by this and thinks his *rebbi* made it up.)

Don't get me wrong; I don't want to quash the children's interest in the Haggadah. But it would be nice if the teachers looked up something new once in a while. That's what *my* teachers did. When I was in sixth grade, I came home with 44 *divrei* Torah, none of which I had ever heard before. I said 22 each night. The next year, my *rebbi* gave me 72 *divrei* Torah, and I proudly told this to my parents, who proudly told my *bubby* and my aunt and uncle, who then got "caught in traffic in front of Shea Stadium on the way to our house for Pesach." Okay, sure. I'm just surprised they didn't think of that sooner.

When I was in 9th grade, my *rebbi* gave us only about six *divrei* Torah, but each one was about fifteen minutes long and required charts and graphs to keep the listeners in the picture. So I got up at the beginning of the Seder and said a *dvar* Torah on *kiddush* that was longer than my *bar mitzvah* speech, until I realized that the only people who were listening were the ones who had paid attention to my *actual* bar mitzvah speech, which were my father, my *rebbi*, and the rabbi of our *shul*, except that the only one of those three who was actually at our Seder was my father. The rest of the table consisted of children, housewives, and tired

Don't Yell Challah

businessmen, and none of them wanted to listen to a *dvar* Torah wherein by the time I'd get to the answer they'd forgotten what the question was in the first place. The wanted short bits that they could understand at ten o'clock at night.

My point is that in my zeal I'd forgotten that there were other kids at the Seder too, and everyone wanted to get things moving so they could actually pay attention to *them*. This was clearly confirmed when someone hid my notes when I got up to wash for *Urchatz*. We can't forget that the Seder is all about the kids, and it is very important to keep it moving despite the fact that we are now quite a few pages into a chapter on the actual Seder, and we haven't even started discussing *kiddush* yet.

Kadesh

The first step of the Seder is "*Kadesh*," which means "to make *kiddush*." ("*Kiddush*" is a noun, "*kadesh*" is a verb, and "*kodesh*" is an adjective. Source: *Webster's Hebrew/English Book of Hebrew Grammar*.) The *kiddush* that we make on Pesach is pretty much along the same lines as the *kiddush* we make every Shabbos, except for four major differences:

1. Everyone at the table gets his or her own cup. This is because we are required to drink four cups of wine in commemoration of the four expressions of redemption that Hashem used when taking us out of Egypt, so we may as well make our *kiddush* count as one of those cups. This is as opposed to the rest of the year, where only the head of the house gets his own cup, which he then doles out generously into a bunch of thimbles. And having one's own cup of wine is a sign of freedom.

Funny You Should Ask

2. As a further sign of freedom, it is recommended that no one fill his or her own cup. Freedom means being able to sit back and watch someone *else* pour you a cup of wine, and then to turn around and pour him a cup right back. (Everyone's cup has to get filled *somehow*.) But you still have the freedom to fill the other person's cup with whichever wine you choose to give him, so that you could have all the good stuff for yourself. But good luck trying to get him to pour it for you.

3. While in some homes the head of the household makes *kiddush* as everyone else stands by, many families have everyone recite the *kiddush* in unison, briefly pausing before each paragraph to make sure that everyone else is going to say it too. You don't want to be the only one launching into, say, *havdallah*, only to have everyone else look at you like, "This is only his first cup, right?"

4. When drinking the wine, everyone is supposed to lean left. Leaning represents freedom, because in the old days only people with money could afford a vertical object that didn't slide around when they leaned against it. I have the same problem when I try to sit up in bed . The bed slowly slides away from the wall until my pillows and I fall backwards through the crack in slow motion. As it is, not everyone at the Seder is able to get an armchair, so a lot of them are going to either be using their neighbors' armchairs or doing that really awkward thing wherein they are leaning against the pillow, but are at the same time straining their backs to keep rigid so that they don't actually put any *weight* on the pillow. Or else they are just trying to lean normally, and pitching backward off the sides of their chairs holding a cup of wine.

Don't Yell Challah

A Tip about Leaning (Har!)

As a lefty, I would like to take the opportunity to point out that leaning left is very awkward for lefties. It seems that there are two reasons that the rabbis suggested that we lean left instead of right. The first is that when someone leans left, he can use his right hand to drink, turn pages, yawn, etc. But if that were the only reason, lefties would be allowed to lean right, and whenever it was time to lean they would all violently clunk heads with the person to their right. But the rabbis also advise leaning left for health reasons. It seems that when you lean right, your food is more likely to travel down your wind pipe, meaning that you will have to try to breathe through your food pipe, which is very difficult and could lead to choking. So lefties have to lean left anyway, and just figure out how to eat with the hand that they're leaning on. Or else they can try to do everything with their right hands, and just sweep the floor under their seats the next morning.

Urchatz

After *kiddush*, we get up and wash our hands, as usual, only this time we do not accompany it with a blessing. This is a really big deal, because as Jews, we generally accompany everything with a blessing. We even bless before blessing. The only reason that we do not recite one at this point is that we are not actually washing for food, but for ritual uncleanliness (and hygiene!). We are about to eat wet vegetables, and in the olden days, people used to wash their hands before wet foods, because forks had not been invented yet, and most people worked out in the fields. The only desk job back then was actually *making* desks, and even then very few people bought them, because there were no desk jobs.

Funny You Should Ask

Karpas

At this point, everyone dips a small piece of vegetable into some salt water and eats it. Different families use different vegetables of course, the more popular ones being parsnips, radishes, onions, potatoes, and parsley. I didn't even know that parsley *was* a vegetable. You can't just say that everything that comes out of the ground is a vegetable. That's like saying that mint leaves are a vegetable, or that parking meters are vegetables.

In the old days, it was a sign of class to eat vegetables before the meal, especially if they were dipped in something. It was like a hors d'oeuvre. A waiter would come around at weddings with a tray, and you'd take a bit of parsley and dip it in some salt water, and then you'd be set until after the *chuppah*. And then you'd use the fancy toothpick to get it out of your teeth.

My family eats potatoes for *karpas*, of course. (In fact, I'm surprised that we don't eat potatoes for *marror* also.) Now maybe it's because I'm starving and I know that there's no food coming for a while, but I happen to think that potatoes in salt water are *awesome*. Every year I eat my tiny piece and I wonder why I don't make it as a snack during the rest of the year. Maybe it's because I don't want to have to wash.

Yachatz

At this point in the Seder, it is customary to uncover the *matzos* and to make sure that there are still three of them. This must be checked periodically throughout the Seder, because *matzos* will sometimes just spontaneously break on their own. Seriously. One year I was holding the *matzos* and reciting the blessing of *Hamotzi*, when all of a sudden, right in the middle of the blessing, a huge piece of my bottom *matzah* plopped off and landed on the table.

Don't Yell Challah

This was followed by a very awkward silence. (It was already silent, because everyone had washed for the *matzah*, but now the silence turned awkward. Sometimes you can just tell.)

The three *matzos* represent absolutely everything in Judaism that there are three of: Kohen, Levi and Yisrael; Avraham, Yitzchak and Yaakov; Pesach, Shavuos and Sukkos; Pesach, *Matzah* and *Marror*, etc. Traditionally, at this part of the Seder, the leader picks up the middle *matzah*, which represents either Levi, Yitzchak, *Matzah*, or the holiday of Shavuos, and breaks it into two perfect pieces, one of which is just slightly larger than the other, and both of which have nice crinkled edges like you would find on a hand saw. That is the tradition, anyway. When *I* try breaking it, the *matzah* either shatters into at least fifteen pieces, or else I accidentally put my finger through it, so that the bigger piece is too large to fit into the *afikoman* bag, and the smaller piece is about the size of my thumb. Either way, the leader then places the smaller shard back between the other *matzos*, and places the larger half into the *afikoman* bag. (In my case, I put a little less than half the shards between the other *matzos*, and the rest of my shards go in the bag.) He then buries the bag deep into his *kittel*, in the vicinity of his armpit.

There are two basic traditions regarding the *afikoman*. In some families, the father hides it, and whichever child finds it first gets to negotiate for a present. I have never personally done it this way, but I suspect three things:

1. The father will hide it on top of a really tall piece of furniture,
2. The children will mess up all of your Pesach cleaning looking for it, and
3. You will not see them for the rest of the Seder.

Funny You Should Ask

The other popular custom is for the kids to somehow pry the *matzah* away from their father, who is guarding it with his life, and to hide it themselves, and then to have *him* look for it. And if he can't find it at one in the morning after two cups of wine, a pound and a half of *matzah* and a three-course meal, he will give up and offer them a present. Or else he will realize that *matzah* is expensive enough without the present, and just eat some spare *matzah* directly out of the box.

When I was growing up, my father never looked for the *matzah*. He only drank wine the one night a year, and after two cups he was afraid to move. Nevertheless, I came up with an increasingly more elaborate hiding place every year, despite the fact that he didn't even find it the year that I left it on a footstool right under the table. One year I hid it inside my box spring through a slit between the bed and the wall. There was no way he could have found it in a million zillion years. I had a whole year to come up with a hiding place, and he had until midnight to find it.

Some homes, though, have a rule that the *matzah* has to be hidden in a lit room, which basically narrows it down to the living room and the dining room and the kitchen, and the room that Bubby is sleeping in that has the Shabbos Lamp. So after about two years, the kids have to start coming up with really creative places to hide it, such as to slide it between the blinds and the window so that *everyone* outside knows where it is but *everyone* inside has no clue, or to take it out of the *afikoman* bag and put it right back in the box with the other *matzos*, or to wear their own *kittels* and bury the *matzah* up in *their* armpits.

All in all, hiding the *afikoman* is a cherished holiday tradition, not passed down from father to son, of course, but more from sibling to sibling, that is not at all considered blackmail, but rather is designed to keep your attention focused on your children in fear

Don't Yell Challah

of having to buy them yet another bike. Children always ask for bikes, because summer is just around the corner, and they totally left last year's bike out in the snow. It also keeps the children awake in anticipation of the present negotiation ceremony, which will in turn keep them awake until the morning *Shema*.

Chapter Ten
Talking Up a Storm

Maggid

Maggid is the meat and potatoes of the Seder. (The actual meat and potatoes come later, during *Shulchan Orech*, but that's not the meat and potatoes of the Seder. That's just meat and potatoes in general.) We recite the Haggadah before eating the meal, because food makes you sleepy, and it's hard enough to stay awake through the meal on a *regular* Shabbos. Also, we can't point to the foods if we ate them already.

In some homes, someone takes the broken piece of *matzah* at this point and parades around with it on his shoulder.

"Where are you coming from?" everyone asks him.

"I'm coming from Mitzrayim," he says.

"And where are you going?" everyone asks him.

"I'm going to Israel," he replies.

Don't Yell Challah

And then everyone says, "Next year in Jerusalem."

In other homes, however, he just walks around with the *matzah*, and there is no dialogue. So you're going to want to make sure that the person walking around with your *matzah* knows about the dialogue thing before engaging him, or else he's just going to answer the questions honestly. He's also going to wonder why everyone's asking him these questions in unison:

"Where are you coming from?"

"What? New Jersey!"

"And where are you going?"

"To get another pillow!"

Also, if one of the kids is sneaking off with the *afikoman* at this point, this ritual is a good way to get him to suddenly freeze in his tracks:

"And where are you going?"

"Um, nowhere."

Ha Lachma Anya

To start off the Haggadah, the leader displays the broken piece of *matzah*, if he still has it, and tells his family, in Aramaic, that it is poor man's bread of the sort that our forefathers ate in Egypt. This is the first reason that we eat *matzah*. Poor people eat *matzah* because a lot of times they haven't eaten for days, and there is no way they're going to set the dough in a bowl on the stove and wait for it to collect air bubbles while their stomachs roar and growl as if any minute a bear is going to come bursting out of their chests and make off with their lone clump of dough. (Nowadays this is not as much of an issue, because we have microwaves that can

Talking Up a Storm

both *freeze* and *burn* an entree at the same time in less than three minutes.)

The leader continues, saying that whoever wants to can join his family for the Seder. It's not too late; they'll have some wine and potato and we'll catch them up. But the truth of the matter is that if someone did suddenly come into the house and sit down at this point, most of us would freak out and try to mace him with the horseradish. You should actually try it once. Go to a Pesach hotel, where everyone is having their Sedarim at separate family tables in a big open room (or so I assume), and wait until one of the families says this part of the Haggadah, and then just sit down next to them and say, with great zeal: "Thank you so much! The food here is *expensive!*" and see what they do. Chances are they'll put on some big fake smiles and try to make polite conversation with you while trying to discreetly ask their spouses who you are, and how come you're acting like you know them.

Finally, we declare that next year we'll be in Jerusalem, so if anyone is hungry they should come now, because soon there's going to be a change of address.

The *Mah Nishtana*

After we discuss our food and our guests and our plans for next year, we cover the *matzos*, bring the Seder plate back into the kitchen, and start pouring each other more wine. This is supposed to arouse further curiosity in our children, but they rarely notice it at all because they're busy refusing to say the *Mah Nishtana*.

The *Mah Nishtana* basically consists of four questions, which are specifically designed to apply to people of all customs:

1. Why do we eat *matzah*?

Don't Yell Challah

2. Why do we eat *marror*?

3. Why do we dip our foods twice? (Note that I did not say, "Why do we double dip?" We don't double dip; we dip *twice*. Double dipping is disgusting.)

4. Why do we lean?

The general tradition is to begin the *Mah Nishtana* with the youngest child, who will refuse to recite it, and instead do that thing that little kids do wherein they frown and tilt their head so that their shoulder goes deep into their ear, and then they make a guttural whiny noise. This is despite the fact that for the past couple of weeks they've been reciting the *Mah Nishtana* at random intervals during the day and night at a noise level that suggested that they were trying to win Color War. They were really excited about the Seder, and they came home from school with their bulging Haggadah notebooks that looked like they basically glued the entire contents of a flea market in there. They have towel-snippet drapes and fake hands on little hinges and an *afikoman* pocket and an enormous amount of cotton balls and pipe cleaners and an actual squashed insect to represent "Locusts." But singing it before Pesach was okay, because no one was listening; as opposed to now, when the eyes of the entire family are on this child, and if he or she makes a mistake everyone will laugh and think it's cute, and they'll keep telling it over as a "cute" story until he's ninety: "Hey, remember the year that Moishy kept saying the same '*Shebchol Haleylos*' over and over and over again? It was like all he wanted to know was how come we eat *matzah*!"

And so it is up to their older siblings to recite the *Mah Nishtana*, which they of course do not want to do, because it's "babyish." Which basically means that they're scared too. The general consensus among older children is that it's way less embarrassing

Talking Up a Storm

to barrel through the questions at a hundred miles per hour like they're being chased by a Pharaoh, or to say it in a foreign language that hopefully no one at the table understands, and therefore no one will know if they make a mistake. Their parents take great pains to explain the entire Haggadah in a way that the children should understand, and the children return the favor by asking the questions in French with an English inflection.

"Papa! Bleh di bleu de blah blah."

"Okay, I'm not sure what you asked, but the answer is that we were slaves to Pharaoh in Egypt."

It's fun to answer questions if you're not entirely sure what was asked. It's like when someone asks you a question really quietly in a noisy room, and you say "What?" and instead of repeating what he said louder or more clearly, the person says it again with exactly the same inflection and volume as he did the first time. So you say it again, but louder: "WHAT?!" And maybe even strain your eyes at him, like it's going to help you hear what he has to say. And once again he repeats his question, just as quietly as before, "bfrm drm sdf, sdflk sdjf sdkjfkjr?" like he thinks you suddenly grew an extra pair of eardrums. But there's only a certain amount of times that you can say "What?" before you begin to feel silly, so at some point you just give up and give him an answer that you hope he is looking for, such as, "Yes," or "No thanks, I'm good," or "About a quarter to eleven," or "We were slaves to Pharaoh in Egypt." Personally, I think the parents should be allowed to answer their children in whichever language they were asked:

"Alright, en Bak kher Per-a'a em Ta-shema'ew; Netjer a'nen en em en pehtey djeret... What, all of a sudden you *don't* speak Egyptian?"

Don't Yell Challah

Some Fun Languages for the *Mah Nishtana*:

- Shakespearean English: "Father! Wherefore and Whatfore is yon knight of Passeth-Over differentst from knights in days' past? Egad!"

- Jewish European Immigrant: "I vant to know vhy every night ve eat bread mit *matzah* mit a shtickle herring and some schnapps, but tonight, just *matzah*! Vhat, everyting else ve don't like? Ve're skin and bones!"

- 1970's: "Duuude! On all these other nights we eat, like, veggies, man! So why on this most radical, most awesome night of the whole year, do we have to eat, like, a big hunk of this nasty white shredded stuff? Bummer!"

- Yeshivish: "Also, I have a *kasha*. It's really two *kashos*. The first *kasha* is why do we *tink* once, and the second *kasha* is why do we *tink nuchamul*? You *farshtay* the *kashos*? You know what it means to *tink*?" ("I *tink* so.")

- White Trash: "Hey! Y'all're havin pillows at the tahyble?! Raht here in the trahyler? Jew hear that, Granma? This is better than NASCAR!"

But there is in fact nothing embarrassing about the four questions. They're not designed to raise panic in small children. They're not meant to be ironic because kids rarely eat the crusts on their bread and never touch their vegetables and dip almost everything in either ketchup or milk and in fact do not sit OR lean, but instead run around the house while you chase them with a chicken leg. In fact, many commentaries say that the *Mah Nishtana* is actually one big question that is supposed to occur to the children naturally:

Talking Up a Storm

"I don't understand: We eat *matzah* and *marror*, which represent slavery, and we dip and lean, which represent freedom. We're free to have other people pour our wine for us, but we're enslaved to pour their wine for *them*. And in the previous paragraph alone, first you said that we used to be slaves, but that now we're free, yet we're still eating the *food* of slaves, but we're free enough to invite guests, but even though *now* we're slaves, next year we'll be free! How much wine did we *have*?"

That is the question of the *Mah Nishtana*. But what is the answer? How will the Haggadah end? Stay tuned for the next exciting section: *AVADIM HAYINU*!

Avadim Hayinu

Avadim Hayinu is basically an abridged version of the answer to the *Mah Nishtana*; that we do things to symbolize both freedom and slavery because many years ago on this very night, at the beginning of the night we were slaves and by the end we were free. This answer is put right up front for the children who have dwindling attention spans. In fact, that's why we have to keep repeating the words when we're singing it:

"*Avadim hayinu – hayinu! L'Pharaoh b'Mitzrayim – b'Mitzrayim!*

Again:

Avadim, hayinu…"

We also put the answer up front for all of those parents who just want to put their kids to bed already, apparently as a punishment for saying the *Mah Nishtana*. "That's enough questions for you, young man; now off to bed." We all care that they ask the questions, but no one seems to care that they get any answers.

Don't Yell Challah

So we give them the short answer, and then we tell them that no matter how much we know the story, and no matter how many years we repeat it, and no matter how many flea market Haggados we bring home from school, it is still very highly recommended that we go on to talk about the Exodus for the entire night, as did the following great Rabbis. Now go to bed.

The Five Rabbis

The Haggadah continues to tell a story about a group of rabbis: Rebbi Elazar, Rebbi Yehoshua, Rebbi Elazar ben Azariah, Rebbi Akiva, and Rebbi Tarfon, who had a Seder together in B'nei Brak, and ended up discussing the Exodus for the entire night of Pesach, until their students came in to inform them that they had missed *Barchu* at the *vasikin minyan*.

I would love to have been a fly on the wall at that Seder. And not just because I am curious as to which one of the Rabbis hid the *afikoman* or asked the *Mah Nishtana*. Their discussions must have been fascinating, to say the least. It's not like they were spending all night discussing the hair in Rebbi Elazar Ben Azariah's beard, or what should be placed on the Seder plate first, the chicken or the egg. And they definitely were not repeating the same seven *divrei* Torah over and over again. Everything they said was fresh and amazing.

"Wow, that's a great *d'var* Torah! What *sefer* is it in?"

"It's not in a *sefer* yet. Do you think I should put it in mine?"

Or maybe they were discussing the content of the next paragraph:

Talking Up a Storm

Rebbi Elazar ben Azariah

Rebbi Elazar Ben Azariah opens his paragraph by lamenting that even though he is like seventy years old, he still cannot for the life of him get anyone to mention the Exodus on a regular basis during the evening *Shema*. A lot of commentaries comment (that's what they do) on the fact that he introduces what he's about to say by announcing his age. Very few people do that. "I am like thirty-two years old. Can you please pass the salt water?"

But in fact, the reason that his age was a big deal is that he was not actually seventy at the time that he said this. He just *looked* seventy. He was actually eighteen.

It seems that Rebbi Elazar Ben Azariah was chosen to be a *Nasi*, or leader, at the age of eighteen, as a result of a lot of politics that I cannot get into. But at the end of the day he was voted Nasi, despite the fact that almost everyone involved was older than he was. This was exactly what his wife told him when he came home that night. So Rebbi Elazar Ben Azariah got scared that no one would respect him, and then he went to bed worried, and when he woke up in the morning, his beard was gray. The idea was that anyone who did not know of his mental prowess would nevertheless respect him, because they would assume that he was seventy.

But maybe Hashem does the same thing nowadays. Whenever we're worried about a job, or a promotion, or a big meeting, or about our children, and we wake up the next morning to find wrinkles on our face or gray hairs in the sink, maybe we're not aging because we're worried. Maybe this is Hashem's way of helping us look older so we can command respect. It's just too bad that when the meeting is over we can't go back to the way we were before.

Don't Yell Challah

So what Rebbi Elazar Ben Azariah is saying is that here he is, looking like he's seventy, and for the past eighteen years give or take he's been trying to get people to mention the Exodus in their evening *Shema*, but no one would hear of it, until Ben Zoma came along and coined the expression, "Who is wise? He who learns from everyone." (Nowadays, children use this axiom as justification for peeking at each other's test papers.)

But why was this so important to him? Some explain that it has to do with the age-old philosophical debate over whether it is better for someone to have an open, obvious money-falling-from-the-sky miracle happen on his account, or whether it is better to have a natural-looking miracle, such as winning the lottery. In other words, if an open miracle happens to you, does that mean that you're so great that Hashem was willing to change the laws of nature, or does it mean that you're really *not* deserving, and by all rights Hashem should not be helping you out, so in order to help you, He had to rewrite His laws just for you.

This is a deep question that has kept many a Talmudic scholar awake at night, when they could have just said the evening *Shema* (with or without the Exodus) and gone to sleep. And in fact, this question pertains to the Exodus itself. The evening part of the Exodus brought some major miracles featuring dead firstborns and sheep and self-proclaimed gods in their pajamas. The day part of the Exodus, on the other hand, was more of a natural miracle; the Jews got their stuff together, they took their paychecks, and they left.

An open miracle on Pesach morning would have been if the Egyptians' valuables had just started raining down on all of the houses marked in sheep's blood, or if the women would have packed only one suitcase and a garment bag like the men did, or

Talking Up a Storm

if the dough would have risen in under eighteen minutes as if it had been sitting on the stove for seventy.

So the question is, does the fact that we mention the Exodus in the morning *Shema* mean that we should also mention it in the evening *Shema*? It would if open miracles were bigger. And Rebbi Elazar Ben Azariah had to believe that open miracles were greater, because at eighteen years old he had just turned into a *Rosh Hayeshiva*. Literally.

The Four Sons

The Haggadah now goes on to talk about the four sons, the basic definition of which is not to be taken literally, because if anyone had four sons with such vastly different personalities, he would long have dropped from exhaustion. The commentaries demonstrate how some of the sons look pretty much alike, but it's just a slight mental or psychological difference that separates them. Yet many of the illustrated Haggados attempt to portray them literally, in part because it's really hard to draw mental and psychological differences.

Most children's Haggados, for example, portray the Wise Son (or *Chacham*) as a boy with *payos* and *tzitzis* hanging out, and who uses his thumb for emphasis when asking questions. Also, he sometimes prefaces what he's going to say with the words: "Did you know." He usually wears glasses, because glasses for some reason indicate wisdom. People who wear glasses are wise. Sometimes you see people wearing contacts, and their eyes are red, and they're weeping, and they're saying to themselves, "If I were smart, I would have worn glasses." This is the type of person the wise son is. The best thing to do with this son is just to answer

Don't Yell Challah

all of his questions, even if they tell you things about yourself that you did not want to know.

The Wicked Son (or *Rasha*), meanwhile, is usually pictured wearing a baseball cap and holding his bat. Clearly, he would rather be somewhere else. The *Rasha* is the kid who ties people's *talleisim* together on Simchas Torah, and who eats gefilte fish before the Rav makes *kiddush*. He doesn't have a Haggadah open in front of him, but he does calmly wait to scoff at the Seder until after you've gotten through the beginning of *Maggid*, and the Wise Son has asked *his* questions. And then he asks why we even bother. Our response is simple: "Hey, can I see that baseball bat for a second?" Let's see him scoff at us without any teeth.

The Simple Son (or *Tam*), according to these *Haggados*, is one of those kids who always has a huge question mark hanging over his head and a blank expression on his face. He would not see a wall coming until well after it hit him. He views the world with one thought running through his mind, and that thought is "Huh?" And you wouldn't tell him to his face, but his Haggadah is upside down. And it's a *picture* Haggadah, so he should be able to tell. To this son you give a simple answer, and then move his grape juice away from the edge of the table.

Finally, The Son Who Does Not Know How To Ask (*She'eyno Yodea Lishol*), is always pictured as a baby with a pacifier and a teddy bear, who has already been put to bed after *Avadim Hayinu*, and we go into his bedroom and tell him a short phrase that he may not understand today, but will hopefully enter his subconscious so that he will someday develop an unexplained fear of baseball bats.

There is also a different school of thought in the illustrated Haggadah community, wherein the Four Sons are actually adults, and they have either all come home for the holidays (some of

Talking Up a Storm

them with new and interesting facial hair), or else they all still live at home and you are constantly wishing that they wouldn't be such extreme personalities so that they can actually find themselves some wives and move out already.

In this version, the Wise Son is on the way to becoming a rabbi, and you can barely even understand his question, and just give him some vague answer about the *afikoman*. If he is worth his salt, he will understand how deep your answer actually is, even if *you* don't.

The Wicked Son is dressed like a gangster from the 1930's, or even earlier, sometimes he shows up with a top hat and a monocle. (Who has *he* been hanging out with?) If glasses represent wisdom, monocles represent villainy. He is also holding a deck of cards, and may be accompanied by two large men named Vito. The best thing to do is to knock out his teeth, and to offer the Vitos some more wine.

The Simple Son is usually overweight, and has potato chip crumbs rolling off his shirt and a glazed look in his eyes like he just played about six months straight worth of video games. As a parent, you have to wave your hand in front of his face until he can focus on it, and then tell him the short version of the Exodus, because his attention span is totally shot.

And the Son Who Does Not Know How to Ask is represented by a mime, or a guy in bib overalls scratching his head, and the way to deal with him is probably to *teach* him how to ask. ("You ask with your thumb; like this.")

There is a *real* explanation, though, and most commentaries offer some version of it, and that is that the Simple Son is considering eventually becoming a Wise Son, but has not yet developed his mind so that he can ask a question that will knock

Don't Yell Challah

you off your chair. He therefore gets a similar answer to the Wise Son, in order to encourage him to keep thinking and to ask longer questions.

The Son Who Does Not Know How to Ask, meanwhile, is on the path to becoming a Wicked Son, but he isn't going to say anything, because he can't hold his own in an argument. And the Wicked Son only ever showed up to the Seder at all because he wants you to admit that you're crazy. In fact, you can't even *argue* with him anymore, because even if he loses he won't admit defeat, and he will just come back with more arguments next year. And if he keeps arguing, you may just lose The One Who Does Not Know How to Ask, with whom you at least have a shot. So your goal is to stop the Wicked Son from talking before he says anything else, and without sending him away and losing any hope of ever getting him back. So you knock out his teeth, and explain to your fourth son why you did that, and then go on with your Seder like nothing has happened, while your Wicked Son struggles with the *matzah*, which he can no longer chew, and the *marror*, which will play havoc with his bruises.

The Very Beginning

Now that we've established why we are having a Seder (we were freed from slavery), as well as who is obligated to have a Seder (even our Rabbis), and when we are obligated to mention our freedom from slavery (every day and possibly every night), and who we are obligated to mention it to (all different types of children, even if we have to knock it into them), we can finally get to conveying the entire story of our Exodus from the very beginning. And the story of our Exodus from Egypt did not actually begin in Egypt (contrary to what you would think from

Talking Up a Storm

reading Chapter 1). It actually began years earlier, with Avraham's father, Terach.

Back in Terach's day, the world was filled with idolatry. Hashem had created the world not twenty generations earlier, and already everyone had forgotten about it. So everyone worshipped statues, pretty much. Some of these statues were big, like the ones on Easter Island, or Stonehenge, or Mount Rushmore, and some statues, such as the iDoll, were small enough to fit on a keychain. It was a very convenient form of religious devotion, and you could bring your gods with you wherever you needed them.

In fact, Terach had a store, called "Terach and Sons," which sold idols and really big hammers, and business was always booming, despite the fact that there was a "Lord and Tailor" across the street, and "Idols Idols Idols" down the block, and an "Oh My God" just around the corner. But Terach had good prices, because his descendants would eventually be Jewish, and he had Guaranteed Overnight Delivery (G.O.D.).

Also, he had wonderful customer service. Someone would come in and say, "I'm looking for a god that will help me in business," and Terach would suggest a big idol in a business suit with his feet up. Or a customer would say, "I'm looking for an idol to watch over my fields," and Terach would suggest one wearing overalls and filled with straw. Or some customer would come in and not be entirely sure of *what* he wanted, so long as it could fit into a small studio apartment, and Terach would ask if he preferred it in black, white, bisque, or stainless steel. And then he would charge the customers tax, and ask if they wanted it gift-wrapped. Then he tried to sell them a warranty. He also gave out a list of requirements with each god, such as which specific religious beliefs the customer would have to keep, and if there were any special holidays, and how often they should water it.

Don't Yell Challah

But there were a lot of responsibilities in running a store, so sometimes Terach had to leave one of his sons in charge while he went to a convention, or met with the guy who was setting up his website. One of his sons, named Avram, was not thrilled to be managing the store, because at three years old, he'd already figured out that the idols didn't really do much, because if the illegal immigrants were putting them together in the back of the store, what could the idols possibly do that the immigrants themselves could not? So Avram went through the whole thought process, and realized that there had to be an omnipotent deity pulling the strings. Nevertheless, Terach occasionally put him in charge of the store, because what did he know? He was three years old!

But it turned out that Avram was not very good for business. For instance, one day an old woman came in and told him that she had to buy a whole stock of new gods, because all of her old ones were stolen. So Avram asked her why she wanted gods that could not protect themselves from theft. And why would someone want to steal a god that could be stolen in the first place? Where's the value in that? Someone did not really think things through. So the woman walked out empty-handed, although she did ask for the name of a good locksmith.

And then one day, while Avram was managing the store, a woman came in and left him a big bowl of flour for the gods. (She had some gods on layaway.) So Avram put the flour in front of the gods and told them that they could have some, so long as they shared and did not make a mess. But none of the idols touched any of it. So Avram picked up a hammer and smashed all of them, and then left the hammer in the hands of the biggest idol.

"Oh my gods!" exclaimed Terach, when he came back and saw his gods. Broken pieces of idols littered the store, and there

Talking Up a Storm

was flour *everywhere*. "What happened?" So Avram explained that they were all fighting over the flour, and the biggest idol had grabbed a hammer and smashed the rest of them to bits. He then directed Terach's attention to the big idol, which had a flour moustache. So Terach took his son to the king, whose job it was to discipline the three year olds.

Avram was brought before King Nimrod, who was a real nimrod, but no one wanted to say so to his face. Nimrod told Avram, "I am a god. Bow to me." So Avram called him on it.

"If you are a god," Avram said, "tell the sun to rise in the west and set in the east."

"It doesn't work that way," Nimrod said.

"Fair enough," Avram said. "So how about instead, you read my mind and tell me what I'm thinking."

The servants all looked at Nimrod expectantly.

"It doesn't work that way," Nimrod said.

"So how *does* it work, exactly?" the servants wanted to know.

"It works like this," Nimrod said. "Throw him in the dungeon!"

So Nimrod's servants threw Avram in the dungeon, each of them secretly wondering how exactly being a god was different from just being a king.

Avram spent the next ten years in time out, which was a huge mistake on Nimrod's part, because it only gave the former more time to think.

"I am a god," Nimrod said to Avram, upon the latter's release. "Bow to me."

But Avram didn't bow.

Don't Yell Challah

"Okay, what part of 'I am a god' did you not understand?" Nimrod wanted to know. This was a legitimate question, because Hashem had just created the concept of different languages, and people were always going over to each other on the street and asking them which part of what they said the others did not understand.

"All right," Nimrod said to Avram. "Don't tell anyone, but between you and me, I worship fire. Fire is powerful. How about you worship fire too?"

"But water can extinguish fire," Avram replied.

"Okay," Nimrod said, "So worship water."

"But water can be carried by clouds," Avram said.

"So worship clouds," Nimrod said. This kid was wearing on his nerves.

"But clouds can be pushed around by air," Avram said.

"So worship air."

"But air can be inhaled and exhaled by man."

"So worship... But man can get burned by fire!" Nimrod yelled, banging his head against the wall in frustration. "I'll demonstrate. Guards! Throw this kid into the fire!"

Nimrod had his servants construct a huge fire and throw Avram in, but Hashem saved him, and he walked out unscathed. And that is how Avram became the father of our people, and why his name was later changed to Avraham to reflect that, and why Hashem chose to put his descendents through the process that would eventually lead to them getting the Torah. And then Avram begat Yitzchak, and Yitzchak begat Yaakov and Eisav, and Yaakov

Talking Up a Storm

begat trouble wherever he went, which is how he eventually ended up in a small suburb of Egypt. But first, a song:

Vehi She'amdah

At this point in the Haggadah, the *matzos* are covered, the cups are raised, and everyone sings *Vehi She'amdah*. Some people forget to cover the *matzos* and don't realize it until afterward, but it's not the end of the world. You'd be surprised how many families perform most of these covering/uncovering/raising/lowering activities about one page too late. "Hey, weren't we supposed to cover the *matzos* back then?" "I don't know; what happened to the Seder plate?" "I think we took that off for the *Mah Nishtana*." And there's always someone who just now realizes, when he lifts up his cup for *Vehi Sheamdah*, that no one has actually refilled it. So we're all in good company.

And that's what *Vehi She'amdah* is all about; that no matter what we do, and no matter how low we sink, and no matter who or what Hashem has to throw at us to get us back on the path, the important thing to remember is that we're all in good company, and that Hashem will always come through for the *B'nei Yisrael* in the end.

Upon finishing the song, everyone lowers their cup, the *matzos* are uncovered, and someone goes into the kitchen to check on the soup.

Tzei Ulmad

The next few pages of the Haggadah contain the entire bulk of the Passover story, the telling of which is supposed to be the entire cornerstone of the night, but from the way people breeze

Don't Yell Challah

through it, it seems more like a mad dash to get to the part of the Haggadah where you spill wine on yourself. This may be the fault of our schoolteachers. Every teacher starts off the Haggadah with about thirty *divrei* Torah on *Ha Lachma Anya*, another twenty on each subsequent piece, and by the time they get to *Tzei Ulmad* they realize it's almost Pesach. So they fly through the rest of *Maggid*, stopping only briefly for *Pesach*, *Matzah*, and *Marror*; *Dayenu*; and to explain what *Detzach Adash B'achav* stands for. It's the same in American History class. The teacher spends the first three months talking about the Native Americans, another two months *each* on the explorers, the Revolutionary War, and the Civil War, and then he realizes that the year is almost over, so he spends the next five weeks rattling off everything that happened from the 1860's up until 1952, when the history book ends.

Basically, *Tzey Ulmad* examines a four-verse summary of the Pesach story that is quoted toward the end of the Torah. The first verse deals with the Jews coming to Egypt, the second refers to the slavery, the third deals with their calling out to Hashem, and the fourth deals with Hashem saving them:

1. THE JEWS COME TO EGYPT:

For the most part, we blame Lavan. Lavan was an evil man who may or may not have been Bilaam (people changed their names like laundry in those days) and who tried on numerous occasions to kill Yaakov, because the latter was his son-in-law. And Yaakov was a yeshiva student trying to support four of Lavan's daughters on a shepherd's salary, watching Lavan's sheep. Lavan tried to poison Eliezer; then he tricked Yaakov into marrying the wrong daughter first (thus causing a lot of sibling rivalry later on); then he chased Yaakov down with the intention of killing him; then he changed his name to Bilaam to improve his credit rating; then he worked as an advisor for Pharaoh, where he kept advising

Talking Up a Storm

the latter to kill babies; then he told Pharaoh to increase the Jews' workload; then he snuck up on the Jews' camp in the desert and tried to curse them, etc. Seriously, this guy needed a hobby.

So Yaakov and his family ended up in Egypt, which was the astrological capital of the world at the time. Pharaoh's astrologers were always staring up at the sky and making vague statements like, "Today is a good day to seize opportunities, and you will also meet someone you haven't seen in a while, depending on how you define 'a while.'" Sometimes they would also get paid in vague terms, such as, "Your check is in the mail."

It was always a good night for stargazing, because it never rained in Egypt. This was not that great as far as famine was concerned, though. So Yaakov blessed Pharaoh, telling him that whenever he passed the Nile, it would overflow. This is why, in all of the pictures in your Hagaddah, you almost never see Pharaoh wearing long pants.

However, Yaakov came in with the intention of leaving as soon as possible, so the Jews for the most part lived in their own suburb and did not assimilate with the Egyptians. They did not speak Egyptian amongst themselves, they didn't dress like Egyptians, and they gave all of their children Jewish names. The latter was probably the most difficult, because they were having six babies at a time—in fact, according to Pharaoh's astrologers, there were almost as many Jews as there were stars in the sky—and there weren't a whole lot of Jewish names to go around back then.

This made Pharaoh very Pharanoid.

2. THE EGYPTIANS ENSLAVE THE JEWS:

So one day Pharaoh woke up on the wrong side of the sarcophagus (that little dangly thing at the back of your throat), and he called together a secret meeting of his most trusted advisors, which we know of because it's right there at the beginning of *Shemos*. He decided that the best way to keep the Jews from building an army of babies and attacking them was to make them work 24/7, doing 48/14 worth of work. He also hired taskmasters to oversee them, but the taskmasters eventually decided that all of that work was too demanding; between watching the Jews mix cement, and watching the Jews carry bricks. So they forced the Jews to watch each other.

But apparently, Pharaoh had never read any history books. If he had, he'd have realized that you don't start up with the Jews, unless you want to wind up with some horrible unexplained illness in the middle of the night.

3. THE JEWS CRY OUT TO HASHEM

So the Jews took whatever time they could find to pray to Hashem, and Hashem of course heard their cries. So one day, Pharaoh's astrologers decided that they had not really earned their pay in a while, and broke the news to Pharaoh that a boy would be born who would lead the Jews out, but they were not sure if he would be Jewish, or Egyptian, or secretly Jewish and raised by Egyptians, or what.

So Pharaoh pretended to pay them, and then he and his advisors went about wondering what to do. Bilaam advised him to kill all of the boys, while Yisro turned to Bilaam and said, "Seriously. What is the matter with you?" Iyov, in the meantime, was silent. He had his own problems to think about. Pharaoh wondered why he'd even invited Iyov in the first place.

Talking Up a Storm

So Pharaoh instructed the country's top midwife, Shifra, to kill all of the baby boys as soon as they were born, before the mothers even realized it. Of course, he had not considered what would happen were Shifra herself to have a baby, but he decided that Shifra was really only one woman, and what were the chances that the agent of redemption would come from her anyway? His mathematicians assured him they were not very big.

Shifra, of course, refused to help Pharaoh, so Pharaoh came up with other ways of getting rid of the babies. So we definitely needed Hashem's help.

4. HASHEM SAVES THE JEWS:

Just as the Jews were about to sink to a spiritual level at which they would have been lost forever, Hashem took them out of Mitzrayim, smiting the Egyptians day and night until they saw blood. And then again until they saw frogs. And then lice. Although Hashem used messengers to communicate with Pharaoh, He alone took us out, using the plagues to prove to Pharaoh once and for all that there is only one G-d, and you do *not* start up with His firstborn. By the end, Pharaoh himself begged the Jews to leave, and the Jews were even able to receive compensation for a couple hundred years of work.

"We don't even *have* that much money," the Egyptians told the Jews, upon receiving the bill.

"Yes you do," the Jews replied. "We do your taxes."

So the Egyptians ended up giving the Jews most of their possessions, including animals, wagons, and their own clothing.

"Ooh," the Jews said unanimously. "Egyptian cotton."

Don't Yell Challah

The *Makkos*

The hundred meter dash that is *Tzei Ulmad* comes to an abrupt halt with the *Makkos*, when, as we mention each plague, we pour a bit of wine out of our cups to show that although we're happy that we got out of Egypt, we're not thrilled that the Egyptians had to suffer for it. The ten *makkos* were as follows:

THE FIRST *MAKKAH*: BLOOD (OR: "THE JEWS INVENT THE BOTTLED WATER INDUSTRY.")

One morning, after three weeks of Moshe and Aharon surprising Pharaoh at the river every morning, Hashem told Aharon to hit the water with his stick. Aharon did so, and all of the water in Egypt turned into blood, the point being to show Pharaoh who was really in charge of the Nile.

Meanwhile, all of the Egyptians were starting their morning routines, when they noticed that the coffee tasted funny. They went to wash out their cups, but the wells were full of blood. So they called their plumbers, who came over and took out their tools and stared down the wells for a couple of hours and charged them a lot of money to tell them that the problem was down at the reservoir. But by then most of the Egyptians had noticed that the blood was actually all over the place. There was blood coming from the walls; blood in the fruits; there was even blood on their toothbrushes. For seven days, they saw blood everywhere they looked. People who went through life proudly announcing at every opportunity that they got sick at the sight of blood spent the whole week on the floor. And all anyone wanted was a drink.

The Egyptians tried digging under the ground to look for fresh water, but all they found was blood, and all of the digging just made them thirstier. They did notice that all of the Jews seemed

Talking Up a Storm

to have fresh water, but when they tried drinking that same water out of the Jews' cups, that too turned into blood. And the Jews weren't happy about sharing their cups with strange Egyptians, because that's a good way to catch a plague.

So some of the Jews came up with the idea of selling bottles of water to the Egyptians at exorbitantly high prices, and were surprised when the Egyptians actually paid for it, but lo and behold, it did not turn into blood. Struggling to think up a name for their product, the Jews decided not to come right out and call their brand "Naive," so they spelled it backward and hoped the Egyptians wouldn't notice. (That joke is as old as Egypt itself, and we apologize.)

Pharaoh looked around at the *makkah* and didn't know whether to be impressed. So he consulted his magicians.

"Should I be impressed?" he asked them.

"Of course not!" they told him. To illustrate their point, they bought water from the Jews and showed Pharaoh that they, too, could transform it into blood.

"That's great!" Pharaoh said, applauding. "So now turn all the blood back into water."

"Yeah," the magicians replied. "We can't do that."

So Pharaoh didn't say anything to Moshe, but he just ignored the plague.

"Hey!" one of the magicians named Larry exclaimed, coming up with what he thought was a great idea. "*You're* the god of the Nile; why don't *you* just change it back?"

To this day no one knows where Larry was buried.

Don't Yell Challah

THE SECOND *MAKKAH:* FROGS (OR: "WOULD YOU LIKE FLIES WITH THAT?")

One morning, after about three more weeks of warning Pharaoh again, Hashem told Aharon to get up extra early and once again hit the water with his stick. Aharon complied, and a massive frog hopped out. The frog looked at Moshe and Aharon, blinked, and then began casually hopping down Main Street toward the palace. This attracted the attention of the Egyptians, because when you're half asleep and you see a frog the size of a water buffalo sail by your third story window at six in the morning, you're going to get up.

Running after the frog, the Egyptians did not know what to do, but they had to do something quick, because it was almost at the palace. Luckily, they all had their magic wands on them. And so, thinking as quickly as they could, they decided that the best course of action would be to whack at it with the wands. That generally works very well with huge animals. But every time they hit it, more frogs popped out of its mouth. After a while they stopped, if only to give themselves a chance to hit all of the other frogs. But every time they hit those, more frogs popped out of their mouths too. If only there were someone in charge who could look at the situation from a third person's point of view and tell them to stop hitting the frogs, for sheep's sake. But that person was still asleep. And chances were he would not make it to the Nile that day.

Pharaoh woke up that morning to find his bed moving across the floor. His eyes jolted open, and he found himself face to face with the biggest frog he had ever seen. Pharaoh rubbed his eyes. The frog blinked.

"Ribbit!" said the frog.

Talking Up a Storm

We don't know what exactly went through Pharaoh's head as he shot through the air at that point, but it definitely wasn't *Modeh ani*.

There were frogs everywhere. They entered all of the Egyptians' houses, parked themselves in their sock drawers, and baked themselves into the Egyptians' bread. But the frogs couldn't die either, so the Egyptians took a lot of Tums that week, which didn't help, because frogs don't like Tums. They wanted bugs. The frogs also made more noise than a house full of sextuplets, so the Egyptians couldn't sleep or have meaningful conversations about how to get rid of the frogs. ("We have to get rid of the frogs!" "What? I can't hear you; we have to get rid of the frogs!") Some people tried glue traps, but that just led to a bunch of angry glue traps hopping around and getting stuck to ceilings, sheep, each other, etc.

So once again, Pharaoh called in his magicians.

"Should I be concerned?" he asked them over the noise, which wasn't easy because he had a frog in his throat.

"Definitely not," his magicians assured him. They proceeded to demonstrate by creating even more frogs.

"What are you doing?" Pharaoh yelled over the din. "You're creating *more* frogs? I thought you would get rid of the ones we had!"

"Yeah," they said. "We can't do that." And all of the magicians lamented on the passing of Larry, because he was the only one who was gutsy and clueless enough to remind Pharaoh that he was the one who was god of the Nile.

Pharaoh summoned Moshe and Aharon. "If you get rid of the frogs," he said, "I will let the Jews go free once and for all." So

Don't Yell Challah

Moshe left the palace and prayed for Mitzrayim, and all of the frogs croaked (so to speak). The noise stopped suddenly, and now all that was left were billions of dead frogs. Even if you liked eating frog's legs, there was no way you could get to all of them in the ten minutes before they went bad in the desert heat without refrigeration. And then they just stank. So the Egyptians had to hire contractors to shovel them out of piles of dead frogs, but it turns out that no other kingdom *wanted* billions of dead frogs in their landfills, so the Egyptians were stuck with them. Plus they had to get a bunch of guys together to pry Pharaoh out from under the big one.

That's a good way to get bugs.

THE THIRD *MAKKAH:* LICE (OR: "THE NIT CHECK LADY EXPLODES.")

For the third *makkah*, Hashem told Moshe and Aharon not to warn Pharaoh at all. It wasn't like Pharaoh was doing anything about the warnings anyway.

So Hashem had Aharon hit the ground with his stick, transforming all of the dust in Egypt into lice to a depth of one *amah*. The lice bit the Egyptians and their animals and their kids until there was nothing left to bite. The Egyptians spent the entire week scratching, and there was no longer such a thing as polite company. Itchy backs were the worst. And *everyone* was affected. Even the lice had lice. Needless to say, there was no school in Egypt that week.

The Egyptians tried combating the lice with all sorts of creams and shampoos, but the lice seemed to like it and wanted more. In the meantime all the Jews were coming up to them and telling

Talking Up a Storm

them that they would not be working anymore due to that fact that there was no longer any dirt in Mitzrayim to work *with*.

"So don't build anything," said the Egyptians, who, at this point, didn't even care. "Come scratch our backs instead." But the Jews said no thanks, because they may have worked in the mud for two hundred years, but they drew the line at scratching their Egyptians' backs.

Pharaoh's called in his magicians, and asked them, between scratching fits, if this was anything to be concerned about. (Apparently even *Pharaoh's* HMO didn't cover real doctors.) The magicians replied that they sadly could not create any lice of their own, although who knows why they would want to. Their reasons were threefold:

1. **There was no dirt left.** And it wasn't like they could just buy some from the Jews.
2. **That said, their feet were not actually touching the ground.** And *every* good magician knows that your feet have to be touching the ground to do magic. This is also the general rule for conducting electricity.
3. **Magic does not affect objects smaller than a grain of barley.** Hey, Pharaoh's magicians didn't make the rules. These rules were invented way back when people first came up with magic. Whoever it was back then could not foresee a situation where anyone would actually *want* to create an object smaller than a grain of barley. Who knew?

So the magicians tucked their tails between their legs and told Pharaoh that this plague was way beyond the realm of magic, and could only be the handiwork of this deity that Aharon was always talking about. But Pharaoh decided that if they knew everything, how come *they* weren't god of the Nile? So he ignored their

Don't Yell Challah

advice, and decided that it was definitely worth it to undergo extreme agony so that he could keep around a bunch of slaves who were no longer working anyway.

THE FOURTH *MAKKAH:* WILD ANIMALS (OR: "ALL YOU CAN EAT EGYPTIAN BUFFET")

Hashem told Moshe and Aharon to start surprising Pharaoh at the Nile again and reminding him that Hashem wanted all the Jews to go free, or else there'd be some serious plaguing going on, this time in the form of the Bronx Zoo. But after three weeks of warning him, it was pretty obvious that Pharaoh had not learned his lesson.

So at Hashem's say-so, millions of animals showed up in Egypt, making their way into the Egyptian's houses with the help of the monkeys, who had figured out how to unlock the doors, and the giant octopi, who had figured out that people would just freak out at the mere sight of them and give up. And if they didn't, the octopi could reach in through the chimneys and unlock the doors too, thereby letting in all of the animals that were too small to just flatten the houses themselves, such as the lions, tigers and bears.

"Oh my!" Pharaoh exclaimed, falling backward into the Nile. A kindly octopus helped him out, and then tried to kill him. Pharaoh ran screaming back toward the palace, with an entire Nile full of deadly sea life on his tail.

Pharaoh got to his palace in one piece and slammed the door, and what he found sitting on his throne was the second biggest frog he had ever seen. And this one had teeth. As it turns out, Hashem had fitted all of the more docile animals with teeth and attitudes. Mad cows roamed the streets, eager to spread their disease if anyone was brave enough to milk them. Sheep mauled

Talking Up a Storm

any pedestrians who could not outrun a sheep. The sheep were supposed to be their gods, for Nile's sake, but it turns out that something bigger was in charge of them. Bigger than sheep, if you can imagine.

In order to give some of the animals the self-confidence they needed to harass the Egyptians, Hashem brought their climates in with them. That way, they could make themselves at home. Thus, if someone was hiding in a closet and it suddenly got really cold, there was a good chance they were about to be attacked by a polar bear. And if the room stank, there was a good chance they'd be attacked by a skunk. And setting out mousetraps just made the kangaroos angry.

Pharaoh called in his remaining magicians. "Can you duplicate this?" he asked them. "Maybe it would help to have some animals on *our* side."

"We can't even try," they told him. "Some llama ate our wands."

So Pharaoh summoned Moshe and Aharon. "Will you take the plague away," he asked them, "if I agree to let you slaughter your sacrifices here in Egypt?"

Moshe and Aharon replied that this may not be a great idea, as their sacrifices were to consist mainly of sheep.

"Not sheep!" Pharaoh exclaimed. "Sheep are our gods!" He watched as his high priest tried to fight off a sheep with a broomstick.

"All right," he said. "I'll give you three days. But don't you go disappearing on some forty-year hike or something."

Don't Yell Challah

Moshe went outside and prayed, and the animals packed up and left Egypt the very next day. And what do you know, Pharaoh changed his mind.

THE FIFTH *MAKKAH*: PESTILENCE (OR: "CAN I HAVE A LIFT? MY CAMEL DIED.")

For three weeks, Moshe and Aharon warned the Egyptians that Hashem would kill all of the domestic animals in their fields.

"But not our sheep," the Egyptians said. "Our sheep are all-powerful. They're tough. Look at that sheep over there; how powerful he is, standing there and chewing on nothing. Bleat, mighty sheep, bleat!"

The sheep just stood there, looking quizzically at them. And then it slumped over, dead.

All over Egypt, domestic animals were dropping like houseflies. Rows of cows waiting to be milked toppled like dominoes. Horses died in mid-gallop, sending their riders headlong into four-way intersections. Traffic was horrible. Mounted police rushed to the scene, dragging their dead horses with them, but there was only so much crowd control they could manage from down on the ground. Emergency Medical Technicians raced around town, but they had no room for anyone in their ambulances once they loaded in their own horses. And by golly those wagons were heavy. The Egyptians really could have benefited had there been some sort of Hatzalah of North Africa or something, but they had never really let the Jews put one together, so the entire Hatzalah consisted of one guy named Shmiel who owned a yellow jacket. And he was busy trying to get some farmer out from under a row of cows.

Some Egyptians, meanwhile, had decided they could outsmart their creator. "Aharon said that all of the animals in the *fields*

Talking Up a Storm

would die," they reasoned, back when Aharon was still running around and warning people. "He said nothing about the animals in people's houses." So they crammed their cows and their chickens and whatever into their one-room houses and lived like that for a week, during which none of their animals died from the smell, because the truth was that the very fact these people would come up with this idea in the first place showed that they believed in Hashem, and that he would actually bring the plague, and so the plague was unnecessary for them.

The others, who had said, "Sure, he brought in animals from all over the world last time, but he probably can't kill a few measly horses," found themselves dragging in their dead animals at the last minute once the plague had started, and spent a week in their one-room houses with their deceased farm animals before noticing when the week was up that it didn't work, and by then they had lice again.

Pharaoh sent out messengers to determine whether this was in fact some sort of *actual* plague wherein even the Jews' animals were dying, but it took him the full week to get an answer because the messengers had to walk. The response he got was that the Jews' animals were still alive, which meant that it really was a *makkah*, at which point Pharaoh said that in that case, he would specifically refuse to let the Jews out. That'll show Hashem.

THE SIXTH *MAKKAH*: BOILS (OR: "HEY, YOU GOT SOMETHING ON YOUR FACE.")

One day, on Hashem's say-so, Moshe and Aharon walked into the palace carrying what appeared to be a bag of ashes. Pharaoh had no idea that they were coming, as Hashem had told them not

Don't Yell Challah

to let him know beforehand, Pharaoh having ignored all of the previous warnings.

"Can I help you?" Pharaoh asked, as the two marched wordlessly into the palace.

Aharon didn't reply. Instead, he opened up his bag. Pharaoh and his magicians peered inside.

"It's full of ashes," Pharaoh's magicians said glumly, because ashes were definitely smaller than barley.

Pharaoh watched as Moshe and Aharon each took two handfuls out of the case. He had to be wondering what they would do next. Carefully, Aharon emptied both of his handfuls into Moshe's upturned palms, and then Moshe condensed them both onto his right one. At this point Moshe was holding four handfuls of ash in one hand. Pharaoh watched them intently, his interest piqued. He hoped they wouldn't throw it at him.

And they didn't. With all of his strength, Moshe heaved the ashes straight up at the sky. The winds then carried them around, scattering them all over Egypt.

"Wonderful," Pharaoh muttered, staring at the gaping hole in the ceiling. By the time it settled down, Pharaoh had ashes in places he didn't even know he had. (Giza, for example.) And then it began.

For an entire week, everyone in Egypt had a skin condition called "*shchin*." Boils, pimples and *tzara'as* graced every inch of their bodies, sometimes fighting each other for space. Do you know how when you get a pimple on the back of your leg it hurts like anything when you try to sit down? Now imagine having pimples, boils, and rotting flesh on both of your legs, your back, your sides, and the soles of your feet. Most of Egypt found

Talking Up a Storm

themselves trying to balance on their two or three unaffected fingers and toes for the entire week. That makes it very hard to get a good night's sleep.

Pharaoh, who, although he had seemingly ignored the *makkos*, did take Bilaam's advice to get a better health plan, tried every skin cream he could get his hands on. He tried *eye of newt*; he tried *wing of bat*; he tried *oil of Olay*; but nothing seemed to work. Not even Advil. Pharaoh once again turned to his advisers, who were sprawled out on the floor in front of him.

"What should I do?" Pharaoh asked.

"Brfrm thlm frfrmm," they advised, their mouths swollen shut.

"I already tried that," Pharaoh mumbled weakly. "It just made it worse."

Pharaoh looked around for his magicians, but they had all taken sick leave on the same day. "Must be something going around," Pharaoh muttered. Hashem had made it so that he was now unable to accept the *makkos* for what they were, as a punishment for refusing to let the Jews out the first five times. Now Pharaoh could not turn back if he wanted to. Which he didn't. Or maybe that was the painkillers talking.

THE SEVENTH *MAKKAH:* HAIL (OR: "CONFUSING THE WEATHERMAN.")

After getting surprised at the river almost every morning for about six months now, Pharaoh decided that he had to do something to outsmart Moshe and Aharon, so that he could read his newspaper in peace. He thought and thought about the problem, and finally he came up with what he thought was an ingenious solution: He would get up earlier. (Pharaoh was not the

Don't Yell Challah

king for nothing, you know.) This plan worked until the first time he tried it, when Moshe and Aharon waltzed up to the palace even earlier than that, catching him on the way out. Someone must have tipped them off. But who? Pharaoh could not concentrate long enough to think about this.

Moshe and Aharon warned Pharaoh that Hashem was going to make it rain, which it almost never did in Mitzrayim. This was going to be a special rain, the likes of which had never been seen before. The rain would prove that Hashem is the all-powerful ruler of the universe. It would prove that Hashem could have wiped out all of the people along with the animals during the pestilence, but that He kept Pharaoh around to show the latter how powerful He is.

Pharaoh scurried off toward the palace gates, where he passed a guard, who was drinking his coffee and reading his horoscope in the paper. The guard stood up as Pharaoh passed. He'd been trained never to ask questions as to where Pharaoh went in the morning, but that small talk was always appreciated.

"Looks like rain," he said.

"You're fired," said Pharaoh.

The next day, on Hashem's say so, Moshe waved his stick toward the sky, and with that, the hail began. This was no ordinary hailstorm. Each stone, which was the size of your head, was made up of a fireball encased in ice. Although normally the fire would have melted the ice, which would have then turned to water and extinguished the fire, leading to ordinary raindrops that were maybe a weird temperature for raindrops, Hashem had the fire and ice work out a deal.

Talking Up a Storm

And so the fire-ice balls rained down on *everyone* and *everything* that was left running for cover outside, leaving the Egyptians frozen on the inside and burnt on the outside, not unlike a microwaved potato knish.

Meanwhile, the Egyptians who believed in Hashem enough to want to protect their assets, but not enough to try to sneak the Jews out, had gathered all of their animals back into their one-room abodes and spent the *entire week* cooped up with a bunch of damp, scared animals. By the end of the week, these people smelled like *shchin*. Lucky for them, the hail kept ripping ventilation holes in the ceiling.

And back inside the palace, Pharaoh spent the entire week walking around with a rain cloud directly over his head. Having had just about enough, he commanded his guards to summon Moshe and Aharon.

"Are you crazy?" The guards asked him. "It's raining outside!"

Eventually, Moshe and Aharon did come back, and they found Pharaoh cowering under his bed.

"Hashem is right," Pharaoh said. "My men and I are wicked. Just get rid of the rain, and I'll let *everyone* leave."

Moshe looked at Pharaoh. Who did he think he was kidding? But Moshe and Aharon left the palace and prayed to Hashem. And once again, the *makkah* stopped.

Pharaoh's magicians called a secret meeting, in which they discussed how this *makkah* was a doozy, and that maybe they really *should* give up, even though the *makkah* was over, and even though this went against domestic policy. Everyone turned to Pharaoh, but Pharaoh was once again in denial, and his mind

Don't Yell Challah

was not even in the meeting. He was looking out the window and smiling to himself.

"Check it out," he said, breaking the silence. "It's a rainbow."

The magicians fainted.

THE EIGHTH *MAKKAH:* LOCUSTS (OR: "GRASSHOPPERS ARE NOT PICKY EATERS.")

"There's a really big *makkah* coming up," Moshe and Aharon said to Pharaoh, who almost fell off his throne because he didn't realize that there was anyone in the hallway.

"What is it this time?" Pharaoh asked. "More lessons? I assure you I will learn nothing."

So Moshe and Aharon told him that Hashem would send a swarm of locusts, the likes of which Pharaoh's fathers and his father's fathers and their fathers had never seen.

Moshe and Aharon walked out of the throne room. Meanwhile, Pharaoh's astrologers approached him, their having come into the throne room because they'd heard that Moshe was around.

"That's it?" said one astrologer named Tupac, who had drawn the short straw. "You're just going to send them back out? We're going to die!"

"It's just locusts," Pharaoh said. "We're all wearing shoes. So, do you have my horoscope for today?"

Tupac recited the horoscope, which made Pharaoh sit straight up in his chair. "Call them back in!" he yelled.

Moshe and Aharon came back in, and Pharaoh made them an offer:

Talking Up a Storm

"Listen," Pharaoh said, leaning over and talking in hushed tones. "You guys want to leave. I don't really want you to leave. So here's the deal: You can leave, take your animals, and slaughter them in the desert. You have three days. But you have to leave your kids here with us.

"Think about it," Pharaoh continued. "You need to run away and slaughter animals. Do you want your kids running with knives? Are they going to slaughter the animals?"

"We need to teach them about Hashem," Moshe explained.

"Forget it," Pharaoh said. "I wasn't going to say anything, but my astrologers have looked into your future, and it's not pretty. Tupac, tell them your prediction."

"Well," Tupac said. "There is a round, red star called *Ra'ah*, which means 'bad' in Hebrew, that is directly over your path in the desert. *Ra'ah* symbolizes blood, which we think means you're going to face a mass slaughtering followed by mourning, which is symbolized by the round shape. Or else it means you're going to face a mass circumcision followed by bagels."

"You see?" Pharaoh said.

But Moshe and Aharon had left.

A few weeks later, Hashem had Moshe once again wave his staff toward the sky, and brought in a massive wind from the east, which blew all night long, and when the Egyptians woke up the next morning they were in the Atlantic.

Okay, not *that* massive. What actually happened was that by morning, the wind had carried in every locust in the world east of Egypt, which we now understand, due to the fact that the Earth is round, to be just about everywhere. Even Egypt, as it turns out, is east of Egypt. That's a lot of grasshoppers.

Don't Yell Challah

The Egyptians woke up that morning to a constant, deafening noise that sounded kind of like a wood chipper, assuming they knew what a wood chipper sounded like. They looked out their windows to find that they couldn't actually *see* out their windows, as the entire country was covered in big, scary locusts, which were eating everything in sight.

"Kill them! Kill them!" their wives yelled, handing them rolled up newspapers. So the Egyptians put on their bathrobes and went outside, because they figured that if the locusts were going to make sure there was no food in Egypt, then they were definitely going to have themselves some locusts for breakfast with the morning paper. (Locusts were a huge delicacy in those days. People pickled them and ate them on special occasions, until somebody figured out that you could also do that with cucumbers.) But little did they know that Hashem had fitted all of the locusts with horns and claws and teeth. So the Egyptians ran screaming back into their houses, and they had to go without food for a while.

Pharaoh, meanwhile, looked outside to see that his wife's rosebushes were slowly getting smaller. "Nononononono!" he yelled. "Does anyone know where Moshe and Aharon went?" His astrologers didn't know, because they specialized in the future.

At Pharaoh's request, Moshe and Aharon prayed to Hashem for the locusts to leave, and a massive western wind came and pulled them all out, until there was not one locust left in Egypt, even ones that had been pickled from before.

THE NINTH *MAKKAH*: DARKNESS (OR: "WHEN THIS *MAKKAH* IS OVER, WE ARE GOING TO THROW OUT THIS COFFEE TABLE!")

"Stretch your staff out toward the sky," Hashem told Moshe one day. "And there will be darkness over all of Egypt."

Talking Up a Storm

As was the case with every third *makkah*, Moshe did not give Pharaoh any clue as to what would happen before the fact. Pharaoh was totally in the dark about this. (Rim shot.) From his prospective, it just suddenly became dark one day. And, for the first couple of seconds, everyone in Egypt thought it was something they did.

"What was that?" Pharaoh asked, thankful that he was not presently down by the river.

"It's a *makkah*," someone said. Pharaoh would have hit him, but he couldn't see where the guy was standing. That's why the guy said it.

The Egyptians spent the next three days and nights wondering whether it was day or night, as well as bumping into each other, tripping over sheep, etc. Some of them tried to light candles and such, but the candles did not seem to give off any light at all, which was just as well, because the Egyptians were trying to strike the wrong end of the match.

The three days of darkness were followed by another three days of an even thicker darkness, the kind in which the Egyptians were literally unable to move. People sitting were unable to stand; people standing were unable to sit. People falling off ladders had three days in which to put their affairs in order before they hit the ground. It was like they'd washed, but hadn't made *Motzi*.

The Egyptians also had time to reflect on the strange sounds they heard coming from all around them; the sound of their closets and drawers opening and closing; the safe behind the painting being fiddled with a little; the sounds of the icebox opening and closing and voices saying, "Hey, there really *is* nothing to eat here." The Egyptians were dying to call out and learn who was prowling around their houses in the middle of the night, or possibly the day, so that they could do some serious thinking about confronting the intruders with a baseball bat.

In actuality, these people were the Jews, sent into the Egyptian's houses with a glowing light around their persons. They were not there to take anything, but to find out where everything was so they could ask for it later, on the way out of Egypt.

Moshe and Aharon came back to the palace, where Pharaoh was eager to see them, having accidentally sat on his crown in the dark three days before the makkah was over. He had another deal to make.

"You can go out into the desert for three days," he told them, because he liked to pretend that he was still in charge at this point. "You can even take your kids. But the animals have to stay here."

Moshe and Aharon were not happy with that at all. "What are we supposed to slaughter?" they wanted to know.

"Look," Pharaoh said. "I made you an offer. If you don't want to take me up on it, you can leave. I don't want to *ever* see your faces *ever* again. Or *else* you will die."

"We've just come to warn you about another *makkah*," Moshe said. "At midnight on Passover, Hashem is going to kill all of the firstborn of Egypt. And then you will personally come and chase us out of the country."

"Passover? When's Passover?"

"I think it comes out on a Thursday this year," said one of his stargazers. It was nice to know the future before anyone else.

Talking Up a Storm

THE TENTH *MAKKAH*: DEATH OF THE FIRSTBORN (OR: "HONEY? SHOULDN'T WE ONLY HAVE *ONE* FIRSTBORN?")

At the stroke of midnight on the fourteenth of Nissan, the plague began. Hashem went over Egypt like a wave, hitting each part just as midnight struck there, killing some of the firstborns and giving others diseases that would kill them in days. The Egyptian idols got hit too, and started smashing or melting or exploding, depending on whether they were stone idols or metal idols or dynamite idols. The wave skipped over the Jewish houses, but the Jews could hear the screams over the sounds of their Seder.

Pharaoh, meanwhile, woke up with a start. He had always gone to sleep early, because he'd had to get up before everyone else to do his thing at the Nile. So he wasn't awake at midnight, even though he knew there was a plague coming. But he thought he heard a noise.

"Bilaam?" he asked. No answer. "Grandma?"

And then he heard the screams. They seemed to be coming from everywhere. His messenger boys ran into his room.

"The firstborn are dying! The firstborn are dying!" they screamed. Society was falling apart.

Pharaoh sat there, unmoving, muttering under his breath. "Moshe will come," he said. "Moshe will come. Stay calm. Moshe will come."

"When?" the messengers asked. "In seven days? You told him not to come back!"

And just then it suddenly dawned on Pharaoh that he was a firstborn, too. *Duh*. That's why his little brother wasn't king. And so he was out of the throne room before the messenger boys could send someone to dress him.

Don't Yell Challah

Pharaoh ran down the dark streets of Mitzrayim toward Goshen, the back of his robe flailing behind him. He had to find Moshe. Where did Moshe live? The palace. No, not the palace, we kicked him out. Midian, then. No, not there either. Lost in thought, Pharaoh took a wrong turn into the idol district, and found that every idol was smashed to bits. And, in the corner, the biggest idol was holding a sledgehammer over his shoulder and grinning.

"Aaaaugh!" Pharaoh screamed, backtracking toward the main road. He took a left onto the expressway and got off at exit 8.

"Moshemoshemoshemoshemoshe," thought Pharaoh.

Pharaoh decided to pull over and ask directions. But there was no one around. Where was everybody? Pharaoh ran on, until he noticed a little boy staring out the window.

"Little boy," Pharaoh began. "Do you know how to get to where Moshe is?"

"Patience, humility, and a lot of good deeds," the boy said. This kid was wise beyond his years. Why he wasn't at the table we don't know. Maybe he was pondering the secrets of the universe or something, while all of the adults were inside arguing over whether their *minhag* was to eat the egg.

Exasperated, Pharaoh kept running. He saw another boy staring at him, his nose against the windowpane.

"Do you know how to get to Moshe?" Pharaoh asked.

"Sure," the boy said. Pharaoh breathed a sigh of relief. "Make a right on Avenue Vav, another right on Mesushelach, another right at the rent-a-camel, and then your first right."

"That will take me back *here*," Pharaoh said.

"Yes," the boy said. "And then you'll ask me again."

Talking Up a Storm

No doubt this kid was standing against the window as a punishment for being wise. Or for stealing the *afikoman* and hiding it in his sister's suitcase.

Pharaoh kept running until he saw another kid staring out the window at him and admiring his footsie pajamas.

"Do you know where Moshe is?" he asked.

"I don't even know *who* Moshe is," the kid said. "Can you repeat the question, though?"

"He's the only one in Goshen with an Egyptian name," Pharaoh said. Boy, these Jews had all *kinds* of children.

"Do *you* know where Moshe is?" he asked the next kid that he saw.

"I'm sorry," the boy said. "I don't speak Egyptian."

"You're speaking it right now!" Pharaoh said.

Pharaoh was about to rip out his last two hairs and run into a brick wall when he finally came across Aharon's house. Moshe and Aharon had set up a whole Seder, and were planning on discussing the redemption until it was time for the morning *Shema*. Pharaoh was about to knock when the door opened, and Pharaoh was left standing there with his fist in the air, blinking in the light from inside.

"You're not Eliyahu Hanavi," someone said.

"You guys have to leave Mitzrayim," Pharaoh said. "Now."

"We're not allowed to leave our houses right now," Moshe said.

"But you're ready to leave," Pharaoh said.

"Hashem said not to go until morning. We don't want to make off like bandits."

Don't Yell Challah

"But you have to go *now*!" Pharaoh yelled, throwing a tantrum in his footsie pajamas. More and more people were starting to look out their windows. Pharaoh heard wailing and screaming coming all the way from Central Mitzrayim. "All the firstborn are dying!" he exclaimed. "And *I'm* a firstborn! Yet, I'm too young to die!"

"If you do what Hashem says, he'll let you live," Moshe advised.

"What do I have to do?" Pharaoh asked.

"Don't back out this time," Moshe said. "Let everyone know that you're letting the Jews out once and for all."

"All right," Pharaoh said. "I'LL LET THE JEWS OUT ONCE AND FOR ALL!" Pharaoh grasped his hands over his mouth when he realized how loud he'd said that last part. Hashem had magnified his voice to travel all over Egypt. Suddenly, the entire Egypt was silent. Everyone turned toward Goshen. You could hear a firstborn drop.

"Just go," Pharaoh wept.

Dayenu

Dayenu is a festive song that everyone loves, although not everyone shows it. For every family that sings the extended *Dayenu* chorus after every single line, there is one family who does it for every fifth verse, one who sings it for just the first and the last verses, and one who starts off singing it for *every* verse, but then gets winded at about verse six, at which point they don't sing it again until the end.

But *Dayenu* is not something to rush through. The point of *Dayenu* is to show Hashem that we appreciate each and every step of what he did for us, and to recognize that each one was a

Talking Up a Storm

separate decision to do something more. For instance, we say that if Hashem would have taken us to Mount Sinai (the mountain, not the hospital) and not given us the Torah, even that would have been enough.

"But then what would have been the point?" you ask, unless you've already heard this one. (My *divrei* Torah are generally not original, as is the tradition.)

The point is that coming to Mount Sinai without getting the Torah would have been like going into a perfume shop without buying any perfume, in that you still come out reeking of perfume, because all of the sales people keep ambushing you and spraying you in the face. So by the time you come out of the store, you smell like some mutant combination of every perfume that they sell. In the same way, there was something about being together as a nation huddled around a mountain in the middle of nowhere that really brought the Jews out as a family, albeit a highly dysfunctional one. And even if we hadn't gotten the Torah, we still would have come out smelling like each other. (In a good way, I mean.)

Rabban Gamliel

One of the most important parts of the Haggadah is the paragraph of Rabban Gamliel, at least according to Rabban Gamliel. Rabban Gamliel always stressed the importance of explaining the reasons behind *Pesach* (the sacrifice), *Matzah* (the bread) and *Marror* (the root).

The *Pesach* is something we used to eat because Hashem skipped over our houses while we were eating it the first time. We were also eating *matzah* and *marror* that first time (perhaps a second reason that we eat *matzah* and *marror* nowadays), and

Don't Yell Challah

the big question is why. The big answer may be that just as we are required nowadays to project ourselves years into the past and imagine the Exodus as if it were happening to us, the Jews of Egypt were required to project themselves one day into the future and imagine it happening to *them*. And that's why they had to eat *matzah* and *marror*, for the same reasons that we do.

The *matzah* is eaten because we were rushed out of Egypt so quickly that there was no time to bake bread. This is actually the third reason that we eat *matzah*. We ate *matzah* for 210 years as slaves, we ate it again at the first Seder in remembrance of the next day, and then we accidentally baked it on the way out of Egypt. We could not get away from *matzah*, apparently. It just stayed with us. Much like nowadays. Come to think of it, maybe the reason that we use three *matzos* is that there are three reasons that we eat matzos.

Marror, meanwhile, is eaten to remember the actual slavery. We normally wouldn't thank Hashem for slavery, but now that we see the end result, we realize that it was all part of the process. And that's why we eat it on Pesach, as well as every Shabbos, on our gefilte fish.

And with that we start *Hallel*, and drink our second cup.

Chapter Eleven
All That and Food Too

Rachtzah

Once *Maggid* is over, you may get up to wash — slowly this time, because you've just had two cups of wine on an empty stomach, unless you count the potato. Once you're up, check the soup and smell the chicken, put the potato *kugel* on top of the potato latkes, and move the roast potatoes closer to the flame near the mashed potatoes. You can also use the opportunity to take the *afikoman* from wherever you told the kids to hide it and put it somewhere else so that if the kids cave, they will not be able to find it either.

After you wash, you're not supposed to say anything until after you've eaten your *matzah*. In fact, based on our observations of many homes throughout the year, it seems that the only word that you're allowed to say is: "new." Why "new"? Nobody can say. But you may repeat this word relentlessly, to convey whichever message you'd like:

Don't Yell Challah

Message:	You may say:
• Bread	New
• Salt	New
• Knife	New
• Stop hitting your brother	New!
• New	New
• New and improved	New!!!
• Old	New
• I said stop hitting him	NEW!!
• Are you finished washing? I would like to make Motzi.	Neeeeeeeeeeewwww!
• Twelve o'clock	Noon
• Horned animal similar to an elk	Gnu

In fact, many commentaries advise that, until after our *korech* sandwiches, we should say only things that are directly related to the *matzah* or the *marror*. "This is nothing compared to last year" is an example of the type of related statement that we are allowed to make.

Motzi-Matzah

"*Motzi*" and "*Matzah*" are actually two steps, but everyone combines them because you can't talk in between. For *Motzi*, the leader of the Seder picks up all three *matzos* and recites the blessing of *Hamotzi*, and then watches as a piece of the bottom *matzah* plops back onto the table. (Okay, so that doesn't happen to most people.) The leader then puts down the rest of his bottom *matzah* and recites the blessing of *Al achilas matzah* over the two upper *matzos*, and then doles them out to his family, who is still laughing because of what happened to the bottom *matzah*.

All That and Food Too

When giving out the *matzah*, keep in mind that there is actually a *shiur* (minimum required amount) of *matzah* that each person should eat, which is basically two large olive's worth. (In the old days, olives and eggs were used for measurements, because baseballs and golf balls had not been invented yet. So when it hailed, they said, "Those hailstones are the size of olives!") But unfortunately, olives aren't flat, except for the ones at the very bottom of the olive press among the toenails and the sock lint, so there's no easy way to tell how much *matzah* actually adds up to two large olive's worth. So the rabbis determined that the *shiur* is actually about 45-50 CCs of *matzah*, assuming that you're taking it through a tube. Otherwise the *shiur* is about two thirds of a square *matzah*, or half of a round one. This may present a problem if your family consists of more than one and a half people.

They say that Rav Moshe Feinstein, of blessed memory, used to divide his children into groups of two, each of whom would get their own set of *matzos* to share. That must have been one scary Seder, as far as being careful not to crack the *matzos*. But I'll bet that *Tzafun* was fun, what with all of those *afikomans*. But what most people do is they keep supplementing *matzos* out of the box, until they forget which one was the original *matzah*.

Marror

Marror also has a *shiur*, unfortunately. A lot of people don't know this, or don't care. Some people take one little strand of horseradish, and then bury it in a mound of *charoses* large enough to pave a driveway, and they're totally missing the point. If they were around in Egypt, they would have come into work in the morning, moved around a few pieces of straw, and then pulled out their *charoses* sandwiches.

Don't Yell Challah

The optimal *shiur* for *marror* is 25-29 CCs of lettuce, or 1.1 fluid ounces of horseradish, or about half of a really disgusting egg. And the idea of the *marror* is to suffer a little, so don't just gulp it down at once, but do try to *keep* it down, and try not to laugh at all of the weird, scrunched-up maroon faces around the table.

Korech

After eating the *matzah* and the *marror* separately, we now use the bottom *matzah* and the second *marror* compartment on the Seder plate to comply with the ruling of Hillel (the Elder), who believed that the Pesach sacrifice was actually eaten with the *matzah* and the *marror*, as a sandwich, named for the Earl of Sandwich, who lived way after Hillel. (Hillel was modest and preferred to be known for his contributions to Judaism rather than his contributions to the fast-food industry.) The Earl used to play a lot of poker, and he hated to break for meals, because he always had the feeling that if he just played one more hand, he would win his kingdom back. Also, poker faces are harder to read when the other guy's chewing. So he figured out that if he stacked his food in a certain way, he could hold his meat and his bread and his vegetables and his *techina* in one hand and his cards in the other hand, and his mead in a can attached to his cap with a straw running down to his mouth.

Technically, though, what Hillel created may not have been a sandwich the way we know it nowadays, because *matzos* back then were soft, like large pitas. So between his meat and his lettuce or horseradish and his *charoses* dressing, Hillel may actually have been eating what we now know as the schwarma, named after the Earl of Schwarma (a large man named Earl Schwarma), who had a restaurant in Boro Park in the late 80s.

All That and Food Too

Shulchan Orech

This is the part of the meal where we get to eat all of the foods that have been smelling up the house for the last few hours, although many of us start it off by eating the egg off our Seder plates, either because that is our custom, or because we're starving and it's sitting right there. The egg that you eat should preferably be about the size of an egg. Less than that is also okay, seeing as about half the population cannot actually swallow a yolk for one reason or other.

But just because we are eating what looks like a regular meal does not mean that it is totally devoid of tradition. For instance, there is a tradition, after each course, for everyone to announce that he or she is not hungry, and for the woman of the house to say: "Well, I've been cooking since Purim, so you're going to eat it." This is because of the other tradition, handed down from mother to daughter, that whoever is cooking for the Seder needs to make a million courses. So everyone is going have to do their best to pack the food in, and then go outside for some air and light heaving, secure in the knowledge that the woman of the house is not going to learn her lesson for the next year, or even necessarily tomorrow night.

Tzafun

After the meal, it is the custom for either the father or the children (or sometimes both, depending on what happened during *Rachtzah*) to get up and search for the *afikoman*, and then to negotiate for a present until about three minutes before *halachic* midnight, (which is about an hour after regular midnight, thanks to Daylight Savings Time), at which point everyone, no matter how close he or she is to bursting, has to stuff another two olives' worth of *matzah* down the hatch like they haven't eaten in a week.

Don't Yell Challah

Some *afikomans* are easier to find than others. One year, when my kids were really little, my wife helped them hide the *afikoman*, probably because she was hoping to negotiate for a night out. I knew that the *matzah* was somewhere in the kitchen, because one can only be so secretive when she's dragging two small children around to help her hide the *matzah*, but that was the last room I was going to search, because I wanted to purposely not find it so that I could teach my children about presents. There was also no way that I was going to ask my kids where it was; especially my son, who, at two years old, had not yet learned about secrets, as was evidenced by the fact that he made a point of announcing when he performed bodily functions. So I got up from the table and started looking around the living room, like I honestly believed that the *matzah* had walked into the living room and hidden itself, and I proceeded to put on a show, for the benefit of the children. "Hmm," I said aloud to myself as I looked in totally ridiculous places, such as under the rug and between the pillows on the couch. "Where did they hide that *matzah*?"

Apparently, this was all the intense interrogation that my son could take. "It's in a box in the kitchen!" he blurted out happily. He definitely did not earn that bike.

(This is why we don't send our two-year olds into battle, despite how much energy they have. As soon as they saw the enemy, they would just start giving out state secrets, before the enemy even has a chance to ask. Also, they would refuse to eat their rations.)

NOTE FOR CHILDREN: When you're negotiating for a present, make sure to ask your parents, as respectfully as you can, exactly when they will be buying you this alleged "present." Some parents will turn present-buying into a Chol Hamoed trip, but some parents will just eat their *matzah* and forget about it. My father-in-law, for example, generally did not remember to buy his children

All That and Food Too

afikoman presents until approximately the following Pesach. So to combat this, my brother-in-law always asked for a new Haggadah. What else would he need the next Pesach?

Barech

Right before *bentching*, the third cup is filled, and a major argument ensues over whether you're supposed to bring the Seder plate back to the table even though you don't really need it any more, and even though it looks pretty sad, like it was attacked by a pack of teenagers. All that's left is the chicken, part of an eggshell, some *marror*, a lot of *charoses*, and a small piece of potato that still has the eye attached. And everything is gracefully slopped over into each other's compartments. Are we supposed to bring it back to the table? The *Haggados* say NOTHING about this.

What the *Haggados* do say, though, is a bunch of *divrei* Torah on *bentching*, like you're going to stop everyone in the middle of *bentching* to read them out loud. ("New! New newnew new newnewnew new…") Chances are, everyone's either concentrating on *bentching*, or absently mouthing the words and wondering if they should have negotiated better, and whether it's too late to also ask for a bike rack.

Hallel

The Open Door

After *bentching*, we drink our third cup of wine, and then immediately pour a fourth cup, generally missing the glass way more than we did with the first three cups. We also pour another cup, called the Cup of Elijah (Eliyahu), and then we open the door for him and say a prayer about Hashem smiting the wicked. On the surface, it seems like Eliyahu is actually supposed to drink from

Don't Yell Challah

the cup, which seems strange when you think about it, because there's no way that an angel would be interested in the four-dollar wine that we set out for him; and, if he was indeed drinking it, by the time he got to the tenth house he would come staggering in, knocking over furniture, and then fall asleep on the couch. And what if you live in an apartment building? Do you have to buzz him in? Or do you just leave a note as to where you hid the Shabbos key, written in Hebrew so that the wicked can't read it? So that's definitely not what's going on.

Also, he is not, as many children believe, drinking a teeny tiny bit out of the top of each cup so he can pace himself for the thousands of houses he's going to visit. When I was little, I was actually *scared* of him, and hid under the table until my aunt closed the door, at which point I would pop out of under the table and point out that there was some wine missing from the cup.

Of course there was wine missing from the cup. There was a kid climbing around and shaking the table.

But the truth is that the reason for the wine is much more complex. We drink the four cups to remember the four expressions of redemption, but the truth is that there was actually a fifth expression, which is not so much about going out of Egypt as it is about going into the Promised Land, the land of milk and honey (which, incidentally, is good for a sore throat). So the real question is whether we should have a fifth cup to commemorate this expression, and no one really knows the answer. So what we do is we fill a fifth cup after we pour the fourth, but we don't drink it, and the basic idea is to wait until the coming of Moshiach, when Eliyahu will be answering all kinds of questions, and there will be a huge line of people all of the way around the world, waiting to ask him questions that they've been wondering for their whole lives, such as "Why don't people who wear glasses need them to see in

All That and Food Too

their dreams?" and "Why does she sell seashells at the seashore, where anyone could just get them for free? Shouldn't she sell them in Minnesota or something?" But we're going to push our way to the front of the line and say: "About that fifth cup, do we drink it? Would *you* like to drink it? Or what?" Thus, we name the cup after him.

Also, Eliyahu doesn't come in through the door. He comes in through the heart.

But why do we open the door, you may ask? That actually might have nothing to do with the cup; it has to do with the story of Yaakov and the blessings, which also happened on Pesach. Yitzchak was old and blind, and he wanted to have a Pesach Seder on his birthday, even though he only had two sons, a *chacham* and a *rasha*. So he asked his son Esav to find him a Pesach sacrifice, and in exchange Yitzchak would give him some blessings, as an *afikoman* gift. But Yitzchak's wife, Rivka, whipped up some sheep and *marror* and *matzah*, possibly in the form of a schwarma, and sent Yaakov in with it, so that he would get the blessings. When Yitzchak was done and had blessed him, Yaakov hid behind the door as Esav came in, lugging his huge dead animal, and then Yaakov slipped out behind him.

So nowadays, as soon as we have finished eating our *afikoman* and *bentching*, we open the door so that the Esavs of the world can come in, and then we smack them in the faces with a prayer about smiting the wicked and their huge raw animals that they drag into our houses that we just cleaned for Pesach.

So really I was right for hiding under the table.

Continuing *Hallel*

At this point we continue reciting *Hallel*, which we have already begun at the end of *Maggid*, starting with a paragraph that discusses how the other nations worship idols of stone; idols that have *eyes*, but they cannot *see*; *ears*, but they cannot *hear*; *feet*, which they cannot *smell*. They can't even swing a hammer.

Some families recite *Hallel* aloud together, as a joyous song of praise to Hashem, while other families decide that it's late and they can barely breathe after all that wine, let alone sing, so everyone just mumbles it at his own pace. And there is always one family member who seems to finish *Hallel* way before everyone else, and we are pretty sure that some of his pages are stuck together, but we don't say anything because we're trying to catch up so that we can drink some more wine and get to…

Nirtzah

There's something about *Nirtzah* that makes you want to dance in the streets. The point of *Nirtzah* is to sing a bunch of songs in order to prolong the highly enjoyable Seder experience, despite the fact that *Adir Hu* seems to attempt to get things over with by subtly cramming about half of the *Alef Bais* into one paragraph. At first glance, these songs seem like a bunch of Hebrew drinking songs, but in reality they are a bunch of Hebrew drinking songs with significant spiritual meaning, although there's no way that you're going to figure out the meaning of all of them at one in the morning after four cups of wine. But maybe we'll touch on a few.

Laylah

The first paragraph, in which every sentence ends in the word "night," an appropriate theme, considering, is actually an alphabetical list of a bunch of significant events that occurred on the night of Pesach. The miracle of Purim, for instance, happened on the night of Pesach. Really.

All That and Food Too

Pesach

In the next song, all of the sentences end with the word "Pesach," another appropriate theme, and cover a lot of significant events that happened on Pesach in general. One such event was when Lot ate *matzah* on Pesach night, and then threw his laundry bag over his shoulder and high-tailed it out of Sodom before Hashem tore it to the ground. Another such event was Avraham's battle against the four kings, which began when a huge giant ran up to Avraham while he was baking *matzos* to inform him that his nephew Lot was captured (he was always getting into *something*, that Lot), in the hopes that Avraham would race off into battle without a plan and get himself killed, and the giant would be left with Avraham's wife, and whatever it was that Avraham was baking. But Hashem was of course on Avraham's side, and Avraham defeated the Kings single-handedly with the help of his servant Eliezer, who had the strength of three hundred and eighteen men and could drive a camel all the way to Padan Aram in a couple of hours.

"What's that you've got baking in the oven?" the giant asked Avraham, as the latter ran to his tent to grab his supplies.

"They're *ugos matzos* (round *matzos*)!" Avraham replied. "I'm eating them to commemorate this date in about four hundred years from now, when Hashem is going to take my children out of Egypt."

"So you're baking *ugos*?" the giant laughed. "That's crazy!"

But as we later found out, it definitely wasn't crazy. And from then on, everyone called the giant "Og" to remind him of the time he put his foot in his mouth about the *ugos*.

Don't Yell Challah

Chad Gadya

The Haggadah ends with the ballad of *Chad Gadya*, which seems to be an exciting children's story for all of the children who are somehow still awake. (Children love stories about animals, even if they're all dead or injured by the end of the story.) But why end with this story? How drunk *are* we? What does a story about the food chain have to do with Pesach? This goat that the narrator's father bought for two *zuzim,* was that an *afikoman* present? Is that a good price for a goat? What did he say when, five minutes after he got home from the store, his son came home with just an empty leash and told him this whole story? Was that kid grounded, or what? And why does the song seem to be written for people with severe Attention Deficit Disorder, or a really bad cell phone connection?

"And then a cat came and ate the goat."

"What goat?"

"The one my father bought for two *zuzim*."

"And then what happened?"

"A dog came and bit the cat."

"What cat?"

"The one that ate the goat."

"There was a goat?"

So most of the commentaries explain that everything in the song is symbolic, with the goat representing everything from Yosef to Yaakov to Moshe to an actual skinned goat that Yaakov served Yitzchak, and that the entire song is a summary of the history of the Jewish people. But that doesn't totally explain why we bring it up on Pesach specifically, or why we close the Seder with it. Of course one can posit that maybe the whole point of the song is

All That and Food Too

that it's open to explanation, and that there is no single correct answer, and that the point of the song is that we should spend the rest of the night trying to figure it out. ("Okay, so you're saying that the dog represents Pharaoh, and the cat represents Nimrod. So who does the goat represent?" "What goat?" "The one my father bought for two *zuzim*." "I don't know; what do the *zuzim* represent?")

Some commentaries, though, pose an interesting explanation as to why it in fact *is* a fitting bookend to the Haggadah. The story of Pesach began with an argument between Avraham and Nimrod as to the correct identity of G-d, in which they decided that man couldn't be G-d, and neither could fire, or water, or clouds, or wind, or man, or fire, or water, or clouds, or wind, etc. So the Haggadah now ends with another conversation, this one between a Jew and the Egyptian who's trying to convince him not to roast his goat.

"But why not?" the Jew asks. "My *father* bought this goat. He paid two whole *zuzim* for it!"

"But the goat is our god," the Egyptian says.

"Why?" the Jew asks him. "Isn't a cat more powerful?"

"Than what?"

"Than a goat."

"Okay, so let's worship cats."

"But a dog can bite a cat."

"What cat?"

"The one that can eat a goat."

"Goat?"

"The one my father bought for two *zuzim*."

Don't Yell Challah

"Oh. So let's worship dogs, then."

"Ah. But what about sticks?"

"Sticks? What sticks?"

And so on and so forth, into the night.

Chapter Twelve
The Rest of Pesach

The thing about the rest of Pesach is that no one really talks about it that much. Even the *halacha seforim*, which go on and on about the laws of *chometz*, cleaning for Pesach, and what to do at the Seder; but when it comes to the rest of *yom tov* they just kind of mention it for a couple of pages, mainly to tell you how many Torah scrolls to use in *shul*, and then they move on to talk about Lag BaOmer.

So in that tradition, I'm pretty much going to do the same thing. But let's just hang in there for another couple of pages, and see if I can't squeeze a few more jokes out of it.

DAY 1 – *Tal*

On the first day of Pesach, we stop asking Hashem for rain, and start asking for dew. Most of us have no real clue what dew is, exactly; we just know that it has something to do with why the newspaper is wet in the morning. We know about Mountain

Don't Yell Challah

Dew, which keeps us awake on Shavuos, but we also know that Mountain Dew is not made out of actual dew scraped off the sides of mountains, although it would help to explain the color. But mainly, most of us figure that the point of asking for dew is mainly that it's not rain.

So on the first day of Pesach, when summer is approaching, the *chazzan* puts on his *kittel* (it's a good idea for him to have a spare *kittel* in case something happens to the one he uses for the Sedarim) and says a prayer that has the word "dew" in it a lot. You'd think that one of us would look it up and find out what dew actually *is*. Maybe *I* should.

Okay, here it is, according to my encyclopedia:

> *"Dew: A thin film of water that has condensed on the surface of objects near the ground. Dew forms when radiational cooling of these objects during the nighttime hours also cools the shallow layer of overlying air in contact with them, causing the condensation of some water vapor. This condensation occurs because the capacity of air to hold water vapor decreases as the air is cooled."*

Aha. That's why you should always use a coaster. But the point is that dew is Hashem's way of cooling and watering the plants without making it rain. No one's basement floods because of the dew; nor does professional baseball ever have dew delays; nor does your mother ever bug you to put on a pair of galoshes because "it's dewy out there." So we see that dew really *is* a blessing, and that's why we have a blessing *for* it.

Also, if you leave your *kittel* on the ground overnight, the dew might wash out the wine stains, and you can then use it in *shul* to bless the dew. Although that might give you grass stains.

The Rest of Pesach

DAY 2 – Counting the *Omer*

On the second night of Pesach, we begin the traditional counting of the *Omer*, except for those of us who forget on the first night. The *Omer* serves to commemorate a time, many years ago, when Jews could actually count to fifty without forgetting any numbers in between. It was also established to commemorate the bringing of the *Omer* sacrifice, and to show our excitement for the holiday of Shavuos, which we are already thinking about on the second day of Pesach.

The rules of counting the *Omer* are very complex. For instance, in order to count with a blessing, you have to be careful not to accidentally count at any point before you're ready to make the blessing. In fact, if someone asks you if you have the day of the *Omer*, you're supposed to say something vague, like, "Yesterday was zero," or "Yesterday was fifty-eight," or "Leave me alone, it's Sukkos." In fact, if you know someone who generally doesn't think before he talks, you have to be careful not to mention the *Omer* at all, because he could very well ruin everyone's chances of counting with a blessing. And definitely don't ask him what *tomorrow* night is, because he's just going to say, "Well, tonight is seven."

Also, even though if you miss counting at night, you can count during the day without a blessing, if you miss an entire day, you cannot say the blessing of the *Omer* until at least the next Pesach. This is especially frustrating when you *daven Maariv* early every night and *Omer* at home, and then you come to *shul* on Shabbos and find out that you've been one day off for about a week. You should probably have some kind of system to remind yourself every night, such as yellow post-it notes on every surface of the house, or an alarm that goes off while you're out

235

Don't Yell Challah

shopping. Women also generally have a hard time remembering, but fortunately they can blame it on their husbands.

The Intermediate Days – Chol Hamoed

Chol Hamoed is a strange, in-between kind of time, where you're not supposed to do weekday things, like laundry or homework, but you're not expected to have more four course meals followed by naps followed by *davening* followed by more four course meals. Also, you're supposed to try to wear Shabbos clothes, assuming you have any left between five days of Shabbos and *yom tov*.

So people find themselves at home with their kids, and many of us decide to use the time to go on family day trips. Some of us even do our day trips in our Shabbos clothes, because there's nothing like holding onto your Borsalino as you go over the loop on a roller coaster, or having a llama sneeze on your suit, or watching your *shaitel* float down the river like a small animal. And some people really desperately *want* to go somewhere, but they can't think of anywhere to go, because they have already done everything within an hour-and-a-half driving radius more times than they care to remember, and they can't really do longer drives because it's already eleven A.M. and they just spent all morning saying, "I don't know, where do *you* want to go?"

So here is a list of ideas. Some of these ideas are not all that exciting, but that is not the purpose of the list. The purpose of the list is to get you there first thing in the morning, so you can be back home again (the main purpose of going is so that you can be back home again) by the time all of the other Jewish families show up, and you can't move due to the sheer number of strollers:

The Rest of Pesach

- **The Genre of Places Where You Walk Around and Look at Various Creatures, and Then They Look at You and Go Back to Sleep.** This includes zoos, aquariums, and the pet store at the mall, all of which are very popular with small children, who cannot actually see the animals because they are shorter than the fences. So you're going to have to spend most of the day holding your kids aloft (not unlike my Kindergarten *rebbi* at the *matzah* bakery), and trying to point out animals that are sleeping way off in the corner of their cages inside a log on top a rock, even though your children clearly do not understand the concept of looking where someone is pointing. One Chol Hamoed we ended up going to three zoos, which is what happens when you try to split up spending Chol Hamoed with different parts of the family. And by the way, it's not a great feeling when you're trying to feed the animals some of your Pesach food, and they won't even look at it.

- **The Genre of Places Where You Walk Around Mainly For the Sake of Walking Around.** This includes walking around a lake and trying to convince your kids that it's a real activity; and taking a nature hike to discover the sights and sounds of nature and families who cannot remember the way back to civilization. (One year my siblings and I went hiking up a mountain, and my brother lost the walkie-talkie that we had been using to communicate with the members of our family who preferred to spend their Chol Hamoed sitting in a valley and waiting for us. It took us a while to find the walkie-talkie, and when we did, we used to it notify everyone down below that we were finally coming down, and that the reason we hadn't been responding to their calls was because we'd lost the radio. "Well, you'd better find it," came the reply.) Also in the "extensive walking" genre is "walking through the

Don't Yell Challah

mall and not buying anything and trying on random fashion accessories and getting sprayed by every perfume in the cosmetics department until you smell like the *moshul* of Har Sinai, and sitting in the massage chairs until the sales staff asks you to leave."

- **The Genre of Places Where Your Family Runs Around and Shoots at Each Other.** This includes laser tag, where you run around to loud music and shoot beams of light at each other, and paintball, where you shoot paint pellets at each other until everyone looks like modern art. These activities help everyone relieve the frustration of being cooped up in a house together for all of *yom tov*: "You kids stop fighting back there. Save it for laser tag."

- **The Genre of Places Where You Look at Things That Are Old and Boring, and In Fact Were Probably Not That Exciting Back When They Were *New*.** This includes "The Museum of Really Old Pots," "The Irving J. Beirach Memorial Museum," and "The Boring Museum," with its collection of drilling equipment. Also included in this category are historic sites and manors, where you can see how people used to live in the olden days, when everything was a pain in the neck, and they did not know how tough they had it because they were just happy that things were easier for them than they were for *their* parents, and they were not even aware that they were living in the olden days. Some of these historic sites also feature people who dress up in two-hundred year old uncomfortable clothing with no zippers and act these things out; you can see them churning butter and making candles; and they really must go home at night with tons of warm butter and lopsided candles, because no one is buying the ones in the gift shop, as most people

The Rest of Pesach

can't afford to eat an entire tub of warm butter unless they are going to work it off churning the next batch.

- **The Genre of Places Where Your Kids Can Run Around and Touch Stuff.** Because of their inquisitive natures, which we talked about at length in the context of the Seder, children like to touch *everything*. So it's generally not a good idea to take them to, say, a museum where everything is hundreds of years old and irreplaceable, or the Museum of Glassware in Corning, New York. Luckily, there are places called children's museums, where the children can touch whatever they want, and the children before them also touched whatever they wanted, and who knows *what* they had. Not that you should let that ruin your *yom tov*.

- **The Genre of Activities Where You Sit on a Boat.** For some reason, we like sitting on boats. A long time ago, before airplanes were invented, people going overseas for *yom tov* would first have to sit on a boat of weeks and weeks and use up all of their sick days at work, and the last thing they wanted to do on Chol Hamoed was sit on another boat. But nowadays people don't usually have to spend a lot of time on boats, unless they like to go whaling, so a lot of us choose to spend some time on such boats as the Staten Island Ferry, despite the fact that it's really just a ferry. To Staten Island.

- **The Genre of Activities Where Someone Will Probably Fall In the Water.** Whitewater rafting in particular is a lot of fun, especially if Pesach falls out early in the rafting season, when the snow has just melted off the mountains and the rapids are huge, except that the water will be approximately the same temperature as the snow; and everyone will shriek every time some water splashes into the boat, and no one will hear the yelps of the person sitting in back as he lands in the water holding his paddle with both hands. If calmer waters suit you more, you can try rowboating, in which everyone impatiently sits still on a small boat and waits for the rower to prove how macho he is by rowing in concentric circles.

- **The Genre of Activities Where You Try to Get Yourself Killed.** Most of these activities, such as parasailing and windsurfing, can get really expensive, so you should only do them if you really *really* want to get yourself killed.

- **The Genre of Activities Where You Hit a Ball, and then Either Run or Walk or Drive Around in a Little Car.** This includes most sports, as well as mini golf and regular-sized golf, which is just like mini golf except that: 1. there are no windmills, and 2. you get to drive around at five miles per hour and look for a tiny ball that you somehow believed you could hit into a little hole in the ground three miles away.

- **The Genre of Activities Where You Spend the Entire Morning Sitting in a Car So That You Can Spend the Whole Afternoon Waiting in Line to Be Able To Sit in an Even Smaller Car That Will Just Go Around in Circles and Not Even Bring You Back Home.** If this genre suits you, but you don't want to spend so much money, you can visit one of your smaller amusement parks, where all of the rides look like you can hook them up to the back of a truck and drive away, and each ride requires you to present at least three tickets, leading us to wonder why they don't just sell the tickets for three times the amount in the first place. But if you would rather spend more money, you

The Rest of Pesach

can go to one of your larger parks, such as "Six Flags over a Large Flat Area," which has state of the art rides based on various themes such as the Himalayas, which looks exactly like what the actual Himalayas would look like if the natives (Himalayans?) suddenly shifted their priorities from trying to find food to selling mugs and snow globes. But if you do go to a larger park, you're going to want to play it down when people ask you what you did there, because you don't want them to know that the highlight of your entire Pesach was shaking hands with Bugs Bunny.

DAY 7 – Gathering at the Water

The seventh day of Pesach is the anniversary of the date the Jews crossed the Red Sea, but we don't commemorate it with a Seder or anything. We do read about it in *shul*, though, and we make a point of mentioning it to our kids. "Today is the day we crossed the *Yam Suf*," we tell them. And that's about it. We make a bigger deal about the New Year for Trees.

But it all depends on your customs. Some Chassidim of Ger gather in shul on the seventh night of Pesach, and pour a barrel of water out on the floor. They then hold up the bottoms of their pants and slosh back and forth through the puddle, all the while singing "*Az Yashir*" (The Song of the Sea). Most years the puddle doesn't usually split, or at least that is my understanding, but occasionally somebody's pants split, or he slips on the wet floor.

There is also another custom, this one performed in Meah Shearim in Israel, where they have figured out how to reenact the splitting of the sea without pouring a barrel of water on the floor of the *shul*. Instead, they all gather together in a dense clot, and then the *rebbi* comes into the room, and the crowd parts to let him through. Then, if there are any Egyptians chasing him, the crowd closes back up on them, tosses them up and down for a while, and sweeps them back out the door.

There is also another custom that I have heard of, but have not verified, in which people gather together in front of a body of water. That's all I've heard. I have no idea where they go from there. Do they wade into the water with their suits on? Do they sing *Az Yashir* and see if any loot spills out onto the riverbank? This isn't clear.

THE LAST DAY – *Neilas Hachag*

Just as we show Hashem how much Yom Kippur means to us by saying a special *"Neilah"* prayer toward the end of the day, we also show Him how much Pesach means to us through a special *"Neilas Hachag,"* in which we sit around in *shul* and share our leftovers and sing generic *yom tov* songs off key. Some people show up with very random leftovers that they don't want to throw out later that night, such as one and a half servings of soup and three quarters of a jar of *charoses*. But mainly everyone brings *matzah*. People who only eat *gebruktz* on the last day come to *shul* hoping to finally sample whatever it is that their *gebruktz*-eating friends have been making such a big deal about, and they find themselves involved in what is basically a huge *matzah* fest. No one can even hear the singing over everybody crunching. I guess that mass crunching of *matzah* is the Pesach version of blowing the *shofar* for *Neilah*.

Chapter Thirteen
It Isn't Over Until About a Week After it's Over

Buying Back Your *Chometz*

Once Pesach is over, you can't just rip open your closets and start pouring raw noodles down your throat like you were just released from a hostage situation in Croatia. (In fact, you probably can't rip your closets open at all. What kind of tape did you use? Maybe a set of car keys will help.) But before you go into your *chometz* closets, you first have to wait a couple of hours until your rabbi tracks down the *goy* he sold it to and buys it back.

"Oh, you're coming to buy it *back*?" the *goy* says, after the rabbi chases him down the road for five blocks and tackles him onto the curb. "I lost it in a poker game." So then the rabbi has to go buy it back from the guy's poker buddies, who are trying to figure out how to redeem an I.O.U. for thirty thousand dollars worth of carbs.

Don't Yell Challah

So you might as well clean up your house in the meantime.

Cleaning Up *From* Pesach

As soon as Pesach is over, your family will divide into two groups. The first group will jump into a car immediately after *havdallah*, and go screeching off to the supermarket, the philosophy being that just because we haven't bought back our *old chometz* yet doesn't mean that we can't buy *new chometz*. The second group, meanwhile, gets to stay behind and undo the Pesach cleaning, which is not nearly as fun as it sounds.

One of the first things you will discover while cleaning up from Pesach is that no matter how well you have scrubbed a table before you covered it with contact paper and sealed it off with 90 layers of tape, when you uncover it a week later you're still going to find dirt on it. Plus there will be sticky stuff from the tape. You also get to discover which kinds of tapes and contact papers can be removed easily, and which ones take off chunks of wallpaper with them. ("Okay, I guess we're leaving the breakfront covered this year.")

It is also your job to decide what to do with all of the Pesach leftovers. My advice is to sell them to a *goy*. But chances are you're going to pull the items out of the fridge one at a time and have the following conversation with the rest of your group:

"Should we throw this out?"

"No, let's save it for Shabbos."

"Should we throw *this* out?"

"No, let's keep it around in case someone wants to nosh on it."

"Should we throw *this* out?"

It Isn't Over Until About a Week After it's Over

"*That* wasn't even good the day we made it. Let's keep it around as a cautionary tale."

I have news for you. No one is going to want to nosh on your leftover Pesach food. Pesach food is only good on Pesach. It has an expiration date of the last day of Pesach. In fact, it's a miracle that it's even still good on the eighth day of Pesach, when all of the similar foods in Israel have already gone bad. Once it's no longer Pesach, no one is going to want to touch your Pesach ketchup and your Pesach artificial mustard and your pizza that was cooked three times and your hot cereal made from sweetened potatoes. You can try to save them all in the freezer, where they will sit like some sad-looking puppy, hoping to get chosen by someone looking to nosh in the middle of the night. ("Let's see… ice cream, microwaveable knishes, frozen pizza… Ooh, we have potato starch cake!") But this will never happen. If anyone were interested in eating Pesach food after Pesach, they would not have jumped into the car so quickly.

More likely, your Pesach food is going to sit in the freezer until some fateful day, about six months later, when you're looking for somewhere to put your Rosh Hashana leftovers (Why do we always assume that we're going to be so hungry on Rosh Hashana after that whole honey-dipping fest?) and you'll find some condensed, rock-hard food substance wrapped in foil that is just taking up room in there, and you'll have no idea what it is, because the label you so helpfully stuck on it will long have come off on the bottom of the fish sticks box, and you will peer at it cautiously and not be able to tell what it used to be, because it will be covered in a six-inch layer of frost (which is frozen dew, by the way), and then you will finally throw it out.

Also, how do you expect to move your Pesach foods into *chometz* containers without making your Pesach containers

Don't Yell Challah

chometz? What kind of counter do you do it on? Do you use a *chometz* spoon or a Pesach spoon? Do you just dump it all on the counter, and then use your bare hand to sweep it off the edge into a *chometz* container?

But what is the alternative? Are you just going to throw the food out? You can't throw out food. We did tell you though, if you remember, that the best foods on Pesach are foods that you can eat all year around. No one is going to complain the next Shabbos if you serve Pesach chicken or potato *kugel* or vegetable soup, because it's regular food. But no, you couldn't live for one week without your so called "staples," so now you're going to be stuck for who-knows-how-long eating your pretend food to make room for your real food. And in the meantime, the rest of your family is poking around the back aisles of the supermarket, looking at the half-price Pesach items they're not going to eat.

"Don't listen to him; he's just a humor book. What does he know?"

Shopping for *Chometz*

The night after Pesach is one of the biggest food-shopping nights of the year for Jews, second only to the Saturday night of the Sym's Bash. That said, I really feel bad for the *goyim*. Most years, I am among the first ones into the supermarket, because I want to avoid the crowds as much as possible, and I see all of these *goyim* walking around, like curious little woodland creatures, wondering: "What's with all the big piles of flour and noodles in the middle of the store? Is there some kind of marathon coming up? Or a tornado?" One of them cautiously approaches a pile and picks up, say, a bottle of ketchup, checks the price again, shrugs, and puts it in his cart. Then I can see him mulling over whether or

It Isn't Over Until About a Week After it's Over

not to take another bottle of ketchup, as he slowly saunters over to the huge mountain of cereal boxes.

These poor guys are there on a regular weeknight because they figure they can have the whole store to themselves, as opposed to a Sunday afternoon, when they have to constantly stop in the middle of random aisles and wait for someone to finish deciding between eight or nine boxes of what is essentially the same cereal, and then continue wheeling his cart down the aisle at a pace so slow it would be quicker if the people behind him would just load him into his cart and give it a good shove. But they have no idea what's about to hit them.

As I am always on the lookout to stem the spread of Anti-Semitism, I want to warn these people: "Run! Save yourselves! Forget the cereal; just get to the checkout! No, don't bother browsing through the leftover Passover foods; they're going to taste a little off! Yeah, I know they're half-price, just leave them! Go!" But that will just make *me* look like a crazy person, and if they do get out of there before the stampede, that's all they're going to be talking about for the rest of the night. "Did you *see* that Jewish guy? He chased us out of the store! That was scary."

So I don't say anything, and they quizzically wander over to the mountain of cereal boxes, and then suddenly the ground starts shaking, items start pitching off the shelves, and the *goyim* look around, like, "What's going on?" And then in the span of maybe ninety seconds, not only is the entire store densely packed to the point that it would take a Rubik's cube expert to get everyone back out, but somehow, within those ninety seconds, the checkout lanes have become full to the point where any one of them is a good forty-five minute wait.

How do these people shop so fast? Are they even *buying* anything? Or did they come out all this way just to stand in line so they can get out of cleaning up from Pesach? That is what I want to know. So much for beating the crowds.

The poor, confused *goyim*, meanwhile, have their own set of questions. In fact, you can see their faces, still frozen in shock. "What's going on?" they're wondering. "How come everyone got all dressed up to go shopping? And why are they all buying the same five items? The prices aren't even that good!"

If they're lucky, some kind-hearted soul will explain to them that no, there is no major Jewish holiday coming up that calls for flour and cereal and noodles with ketchup, but that we are buying these foods because Pesach is over. And no, the prices aren't even all that good.

The Shabbos After Pesach

The Shabbos after Pesach is pretty much a normal Shabbos, except, of course, for the Pesach leftovers, and the fact that many of us bake a key into the *challah*. Yes, right into the *challah*. As if we're helping someone break out of jail. This is an old tradition that has many different reasons, but most of them boil down to it being an omen for *parnassah* (livelihood).

We're Jews. *Everything* we do is an omen for *parnassah*.

There is an actual connection to *parnassah* here, though. When the Jews were in the desert for forty years, they didn't have to work for a living; they got their food in the form of *mann* (or *manna*), which fell from the sky every morning, and could taste like whatever they imagined, although you have to realize that they didn't have pizza and ice cream back then, so their imagination was pretty much limited to bread and produce. But when they came into the Promised Land after the Pesach of the fortieth year, the *mann* (*manna*) stopped falling, and in order to

It Isn't Over Until About a Week After it's Over

get food they had to rely on a combination of merit and elbow grease. The elbow grease they could manage, but merit would be decided by Hashem, who keeps it behind the metaphorical "Gates of Livelihood." The purpose of baking a key into our *challah* is to open up those gates, so you can afford to totally restock your house with food.

But before you go loading up your *challah* with whatever you can get your hands on (i.e. the key to the top lock, the key to the bottom lock, the one attached to your tie clip, the little beepy thing from your car, your garage door opener, the combination of your Shabbos lock scratched into the bottom of the *challah*), so that it ends up weighing ten pounds and is a veritable landmine of things you don't want to bite into, lest you spend most of your *parnassah* at the dentist, bear in mind that:

1. There really is only one gate of livelihood, with only one metaphorical keyhole (Hashem doesn't live in a bad neighborhood), and chances are that none of your keys will *actually* fit the lock anyway. It's all a symbolic prayer anyhow, so it's really just as effective to put in one key.

2. That said, it should be an actual working key. Don't put in a key that you found during Pesach cleaning that you have no idea what it does.

3. But if you do, make sure to wash it first.

On the other hand, if you're planning on purchasing your *challah* from the bakery, don't expect a free key. Chances are that the bakery is not going to put keys in their *challos*. Which key would they use? Should they just make copies of the key to the front door, and have *chometz*-starved people walk in on Shabbos afternoon, looking for cookies? However, they might perform one of the other key-related traditions, which include poking the dough with a key before sticking it into the oven, baking a small, key-shaped piece of dough on *top* of the challah, and making the entire challah in the shape of a key, like it's the key to your stomach.

Once again, it all boils down to customs. In fact, most of Pesach boils down to customs. Customs don't always make sense, and sometimes they are so vastly different from each other so that it's hard to believe that they both came from the same religion. Plus, a lot of the things we do aren't even necessarily customs at all.

My mother-in-law tells a story, way too often, about a supposedly non-Jewish girl who lit candles in her bedroom closet every Friday night. When people asked her why she did this, she said that her great-grandmother used to do the same thing in the old country. Apparently, this woman was trying to hide her religion, and she did it so well that her own grandchildren didn't know they were Jewish. They just thought that making a fire hazard in the closet once a week was a family tradition, rather than a practicality of the time. Sometimes people do things for practical reasons that apply to themselves only, rather than for the sake of a family tradition. "Do we eat the egg off the Seder plate?" "I don't know; Grandpa doesn't eat the egg." Well, maybe he doesn't eat the egg because it's bad for his cholesterol.

We can't always simply watch what our elders do and mimic them. We have to communicate with them; to ask them why they do the things that they do. Maybe the reason that Hashem has allowed Pesach to turn into such a confusing organism with so many varied traditions that are so complicated and diverse was to foster communication between parents and their children. Because when it comes to your family's Pesach traditions, there is only one place you can go to ask.

"Hey Abba, about the egg; do we eat it?"

It Isn't Over Until About a Week After it's Over

"Yes, we eat it! I just don't like eggs."

Maybe that's what Pesach is all about.

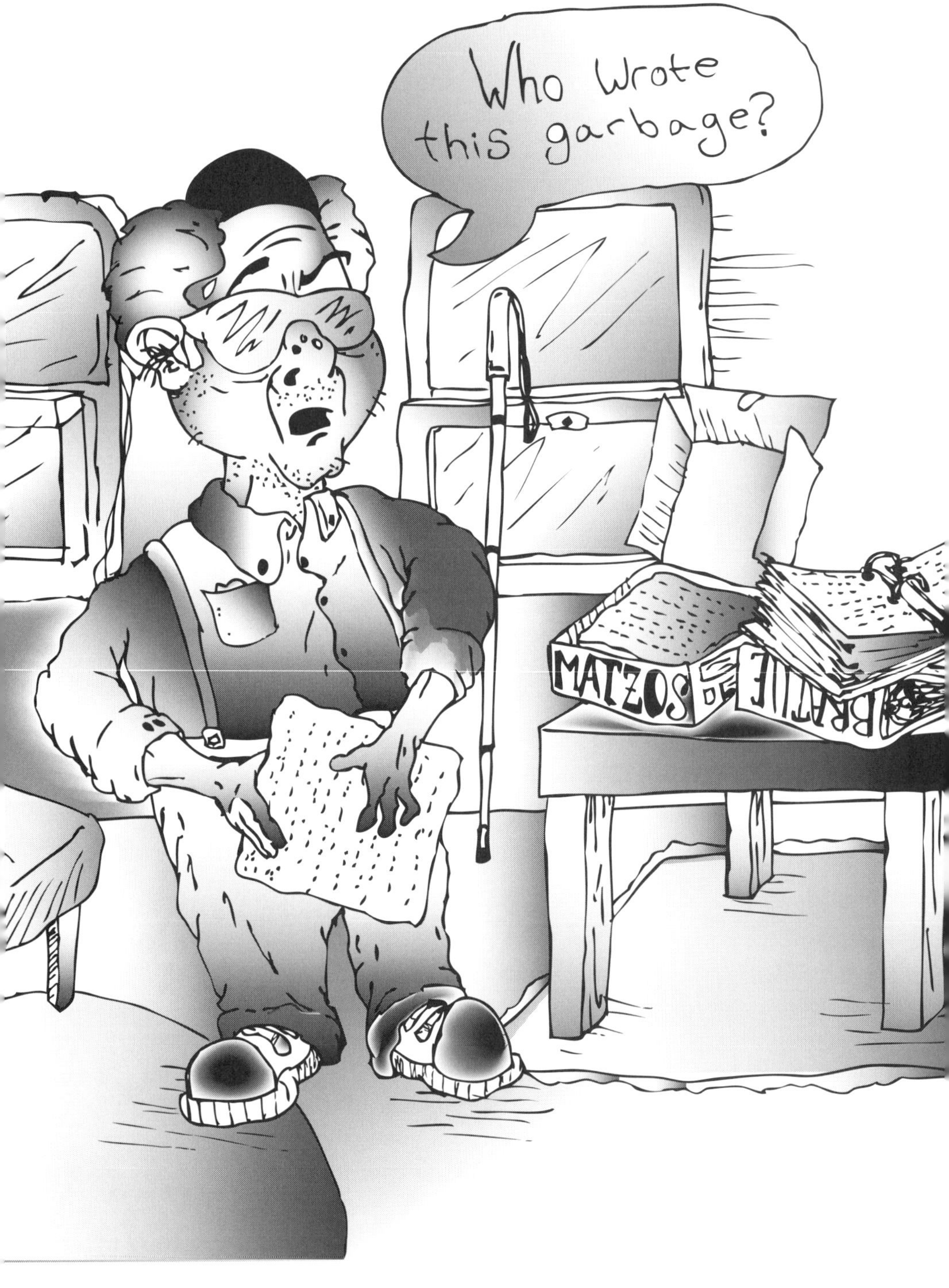
Who wrote this garbage?
MATZOS

About the Author

Mordechai Schmutter writes a weekly humor column for Hamodia, which **CENSORED BY HAMODIA** He also teaches Language Arts in a yeshiva high school, where he tries to get kids to stop saying, "He's staying by me in the house." But it's an uphill battle. He lives in New Jersey with his wife and kids. This is his first book. That he has written.